World Energy Markets and OPEC Stability

World Energy Markets and OPEC Stability

Ali Ezzati
Brookhaven National Laboratory

Lexington Books
D.C. Heath and Company
Lexington, Massachusetts
Toronto

Library of Congress Cataloging in Publication Data

Ezzati, Ali.
    World energy markets and OPEC stability.

    Bibliography: p.
    Includes index.
    1. Energy policy. 2. Petroleum industry and trade. 3. Organization
of Petroleum Exporting countries.
I. Title.
HD9502.A2E98   333.7   77-14615
ISBN 0-669-01950-X

Published simultaneously in Canada.

Printed in the United States of America.

International Standard Book Number: 0-669-01950-X

Library of Congress Catalog Card Number: 77-14615

To Trena, Mitra, and Alan

Contents

List of Figures

List of Tables

Preface

This book presents an analytical framework for evaluating energy policy issues concerning world energy markets. The framework is designed to closely approximate the behavior of all important aspects of those markets. Equilibrium prices, supply, demand, imports, and exports of alternative forms of energy can be determined for each of the major regions of the world. The interaction of oil-importing and -producing countries can be evaluated, and OPEC price and production strategies can be identified and forecasted under alternative sets of conditions.

Originally I developed an interest in constructing a world energy modeling framework in 1969 when I was at Indiana University working toward a Ph.D. degree. I developed a generalized version of a segment of the framework for my dissertation. Then I joined Gulf Oil Corporation where I was actively involved in its worldwide corporate planning models. I benefited extensively from work already in existence and from the ideas of my colleagues as to how real world energy markets operate in developing the conceptual framework for a world energy model. Then I accepted a position with the Federal Energy Administration (FEA), now the Department of Energy, as chief of its International Energy Modeling and Forecasting Division, a most appropriate place for implementing the conceptual framework developed over many years. During this period, I benefited extensively from the work done by my colleagues on the Project Independence Evaluation System (PIES) and from the works of others, both within and outside the agency. PIES was utilized to generate some of the input data used in this book. The manuscript was completed prior to my joining the Brookhaven National Laboratory.

This book reflects the assistance and contributions of many individuals to whom I am greatly indebted. Above all, I am indebted to Gerard L. Lagace of the Federal Energy Administration for his extensive review, valuable comments, and continous encouragement, without which this book would not have been completed. The book has been extensively restructured and its scope extended as a result of his suggestions. His review has improved both the analysis and the exposition.

I would also like to thank F. Gerard Adams and James Griffin for making their OECD demand model available for inclusion in the actual programmed version of the world energy model, as well as in this book. I am indebted to William Hogan for his inspiration during my association with him at the Federal Energy Administration and his ideas on the Project Independence Evaluation System. I have also benefited from the ideas of Ragai El-Mallakh, Hendrik Houthakker, Michael Kennedy, Milton Russell, Thomas Sparrow, Cecil Thompson and Jean Waelbroeck. I am indebted to my former colleagues in the International Energy Modeling and

Forecasting Division of FEA, Patricia Baade, Stuart Edwards, Charles Everett, Webster Kilgore, and Ercan Tukenmez, whose efforts contributed to the development of the world energy model presented in this book. I am also indebted to Paul Hurley and Arlene Ryan who assisted me in constructing the OPEC oil supply model component of the world energy model, an initial version of which was published in the *European Economic Review*.

I would like to thank Bonner and Moore Associates, Inc., particularly John Bonner and Frank Frederick, for their interest and cooperation in developing the generalized computer software used for the world energy model. I am indebted to the staff of ICF, Inc., for many of their ideas on the Project Independence Evaluation System and to John Pearson for following up on development of the model at FEA. Norma Dosky has earned my deep gratitude for her superior and constant performance in typing the final draft of the manuscript for the publisher.

I am indebted to my former colleagues at Gulf Oil Corporation, including Warren Davis and Mark Owings; to my thesis advisers at Indiana University, Franz Gehrels, George Stolnitz, Richard Farmer, and William Perkins; and to Jeffrey Green for introducing me to quantitative modeling. Finally, I am indebted to my wife and children who made the greatest sacrifice and to whom this book is dedicated.

**Part I
The World Energy Economy**

1

Introduction

Dramatic changes have occurred in world energy markets during the 1970s compared to the relatively stable environment of prior decades. The Organization of Petroleum Exporting Countries (OPEC)[1] has become the major force in determining the crude oil price and production policies of its members and in revolutionizing contractual relationships with the international oil companies. As a result, the traditional role of the major international oil companies as the sole power in international petroleum market activities (exploration, production, transportation, refining, and marketing) has changed. The domestic pricing and energy resource development policies of oil-importing countries as well as their energy consumption patterns have also changed. Massive transfers of wealth from the major industrial countries to the OPEC member countries have occurred. Concern over balance-of-payments deficits and recycling of surplus revenues back to the economies of the industrial countries has intensified. New economic relationships are emerging between the developed industrial countries, OPEC member countries, and other underdeveloped countries. These new relationships have been accompanied by a new era of international diplomacy.

Since 1971, OPEC has altered the energy market by increasing the prices of its crude oil and the degree to which it participates in domestic petroleum operations. During the 1960s, OPEC countries had usually increased their revenues by increasing their production and, occasionally, their taxes. In 1971 and 1972, the world oil surplus was reduced in relation to world demand for petroleum. At the same time, OPEC production declined as a result of a series of political actions and production decisions by Iraq, Libya, and Kuwait. The world petroleum market, which had been a buyer's market for a decade, was rapidly transformed into a seller's market, which enabled the oil-producing countries and the national oil companies of these nations to secure greater control over their markets. Not only did OPEC countries increase taxes during these early years of the 1970s, but they also increased their participation in their domestic petroleum operations. This was the situation when war started in the Middle East in late 1973 and an embargo was imposed on the United States by the Arab countries. OPEC countries then quadrupled their crude oil prices and accelerated the nationalization of oil operations. These changes give OPEC control over and responsibility for producing enough oil to balance the world demand for and non-OPEC supply of energy. Importing countries must now adjust

1

their energy consumption to levels consistent with oil volumes that OPEC makes available and at prices that it sets.

Oil-producing countries' control over their domestic oil operations and the involvement of state-owned corporations in managing these operations have substantially changed the role of private oil companies in the international energy markets. In most cases, private oil companies have lost both the ownership of crude oil reserves and the power to set crude oil prices and production volumes. But they still control and play an important role in much of the transportation and downstream refining and marketing activities. They also retain overwhelming strength in technical know-how and management expertise.

OPEC's proved petroleum reserves in 1976 were estimated to be more than 500 billion barrels, or about 85 percent of proven noncommunist world oil reserves. OPEC production in 1976 constituted about 65 percent of noncommunist production.

Prices of OPEC oil have changed greatly. Posted prices for Saudi Arabian light crude, the so-called marker crude, were relatively stable at $1.25 to $2.60 per barrel from 1950 to 1972. However, by late 1973, OPEC countries unilaterally increased posted prices of marker crude to $5.12 per barrel and by July 1977 to $12.70.

The rapid increase in oil prices generated a massive amount of oil revenues for OPEC member countries. Government takes from oil exports amounted to about $98 billion in 1975, and in 1976 they were about $111 billion.[2] The potential transfer of such a large sum from oil-importing to oil-exporting countries initially created some concern on the part of the major industrial countries. A related concern was the apparent inability of the major oil-producing countries to absorb these oil revenues. The passage of time has shown that the transfer of such sums is manageable and does not damage the economies of the industrial countries. However, the limited capacity of some OPEC members to absorb oil revenues is still of major concern and is a major determinant of OPEC's future price and production strategies. Limited absorptive capacity may lead to cutbacks in production and to eventual higher prices; the need for greater oil revenues by those members with higher absorptive capacities may lead to greater production and eventual downward pressure on world crude oil prices. Algeria, Indonesia, and Nigeria can absorb prospective oil revenues. Iran, Iraq, and Venezuela have short-term limitations in absorbing their oil revenues; but as their ambitious economic development plans are implemented, their surplus revenues will rapidly decrease. Saudi Arabia, Kuwait, the United Arab Emirates, and Libya have large oil reserves and limited absorptive capacity; thus they will have substantial surpluses of petrodollars.

The increase in petroleum prices may eventually reduce the demand for OPEC oil by reducing world demand for and increasing world production of petroleum and other energy resources. Allocation of demand for OPEC oil among its members may create conflict between members of high and low absorptive and productive capacity. Thus, OPEC's future stability and its price and production strategies may require an effective production prorationing scheme. OPEC's share in total world oil reserves and the amount of revenues that are projected to flow to it will significantly influence these strategies, since they will affect the rate of growth of the world economy, worldwide income distribution, the level and allocation of investment, world money, and capital markets as well as the patterns of development within countries. OPEC members will therefore need to balance their price and production decisions in order to avoid disrupting the world economy, to maintain their revenues at levels adequate to finance domestic growth, and to maintain good relations among themselves.

The factors which will shape world energy markets in the future are possible discoveries of large reserves of oil, new sources of energy, energy conservation measures, OPEC's price-production strategies and the absorptive capacity of its members, economic growth and demand for energy products in oil-importing countries, and the ability of oil-importing countries to control their balance-of-payments deficits at manageable levels.

The role of new petroleum reserves and new energy sources is significant for the future structure and balance of the world energy market. The discoveries in the North Sea, Alaska, offshore Mexico, Brazil, the South China Sea, Russia, and China may change the pattern of world trade in petroleum to some extent. The introduction of new sources of energy, such as tar sands, oil shale, and solar and nuclear energy on a basis competitive with crude oil prices, could change the shares and components of various forms of energy in the world market. Depending on the price at which substitution of OPEC oil for other sources of energy takes place and the degree and speed at which substitution occurs, OPEC's price and production decisions could have a major impact on world energy demand and supply, the level and composition of energy-related investments, and the levels of OPEC countries' revenues.

The rate of substitution between different forms of energy does not depend solely on OPEC decisions. There is still a substantial margin between OPEC prices and prices that consumers pay for oil. Governments of oil-consuming countries may keep prices high through taxation and encourage substitution irrespective of OPEC price and production policies. Such policies could result in a loss of revenues to OPEC countries.

World demand for energy is highly correlated with economic growth, the level of energy conservation, and OPEC's price strategy. A great effort has been made to reduce petroleum consumption through conservation, and there is still substantial potential for further reduction in transportation, residential, and industrial consumption. Price strategies on the part of OPEC and tax strategies by governments of oil-importing countries have dampened the demand for petroleum products. The United States, which for many years had access to inexpensive and ample supplies of energy, is now facing a period where growth in energy demand is accompanied by growing supply problems. These problems are the result of a decline in proved domestic reserves of oil and gas and environmental constraints, which have led to increased energy imports. Even with the North Sea discoveries, Europe will be dependent on oil imports for the majority of its oil requirements. In 1976, about 95 percent of Europe's oil requirements were satisfied by oil imported from OPEC countries. Japan is most dependent of all, and almost all its demand for petroleum must be satisfied with imported oil.

The ever-increasing dependence of oil-importing countries on OPEC is of major concern to these countries. The main concern is the security of foreign sources of supply. There are no substantial quantities of non-OPEC oil presently available for export. Diversification between energy forms does not provide the industrialized countries with a viable alternative either. The coal industry is continuously under pressure of rising costs and workforce shortages. The demand for natural gas, which has an expanding use as a raw material for the manufacture of petrochemicals, cannot be fully supplied from indigenous sources. Imported liquified natural gas is very costly, and there is little flexibility in sources of supply. Oil shale, tar sands, coal liquefaction, and coal gasification are still in the development stage. Similarly, thus far nuclear power has not been able to capture a substantial portion of the energy market. The emerging pattern seems to be one of increased dependence on imported oil for the industrialized countries.

The oil-importing countries have reacted differently to higher oil prices depending on the relative availability of indigenous energy resources and degree of dependency on imported oil. Imported oil constitutes about 63 percent of total energy needs in Western Europe and about 80 and 18 percent for Japan and the United States, respectively.

What problems do the oil-importing countries face? The main problems are how to maintain their economic growth, how to pay for high-priced imported oil, how to increase the security of foreign sources of supply, and how to develop more indigenous energy resources. Increased conservation and improved efficiency in fuel use were the first steps taken to alleviate some of the problems. Stockpiling and other emergency measures are being adopted by some countries in order to minimize the impact of embargoes on their economic activity. Substantial effort and investment are being devoted to developing alternative energy resources and to increasing domestic recoverable reserves of oil and gas. The efforts being made to discover and develop new oil and gas reserves are focused outside the OPEC area, such as the North Sea, the Arctic regions, offshore United States east and west coasts, offshore Mexico and Brazil, and the various regions of the Far East. Efforts to develop alternative resources are focused on coal gasification, oil shale, tar sands, and solar and nuclear energy. Finally, the high prices of petroleum products together with mandatory conservation measures have induced substantial reductions in demand in major industrial countries.

The development of indigenous energy resources and the attainment of higher degrees of energy self-sufficiency by oil-importing countries require a systematic monitoring and prediction of world energy balances and energy economics. Forecasts of future crude oil prices, crude oil availability, OPEC's stability, and its price and production strategies all affect the decisions of oil-importing countries with respect to developing alternative and costlier energy resources. These decisions affect their economies. The size of the bill for imported oil could create potentially large deficits in the balance of payments of importing countries and thereby induce additional efforts to expand exports to OPEC member countries in order to attract petrodollars. Thus, forecasts of surplus petrodollars, their international flow, and balance-of-payments deficits should be made. Further, if the objectives of oil-importing countries are to be attained, forecasts of prices, supply, demand, imports, and exports of petroleum products and other energy forms in various regions of the world are required. Energy imports by area of origin determine the vulnerability and dependency of oil-importing countries on particular countries. This dependency is based on present and future world refining and production capacities and on the responsiveness of consumption patterns to higher prices and to conservation measures.

The future power of OPEC member countries is dependent upon their future capacity to absorb oil revenues, their ability to maintain unified price and production strategies, their ability to implement an effective and reasonable production prorationing scheme, the rate of growth of their economies, the impact of higher oil prices on world demand and non-OPEC supplies, investment of surplus petrodollars in foreign countries, and the amount of oil revenues needed for developmental programs.

The problems which concern both the oil-importing and the oil-exporting countries are highly interrelated and should be analyzed within an integrated framework. As a matter of fact, the oil-importing countries and the OPEC member countries look at the same questions and problems about the world energy market but from two different perspectives.

This book presents an analytical framework for evaluating these questions and problems from the perspectives of both the oil-importing and OPEC countries. A world energy model consistent with the framework is constructed to facilitate analysis. The model is then used to analyze the world energy market for the 1975-1985 period. It provides for the simultaneous interaction and determination of price, supply, demand, imports, and exports of oil and other energy forms in different regions under equilibrium conditions. It also provides for the technology of exploration, production, transportation, refining, and other energy conversion processes. Further, it establishes the feedback relationships between the structure of the world energy market and related variables, on the one hand, and the national economies of different countries, on the other. The price, production, and domestic and foreign investment strategies of OPEC countries, as they relate to their economic growth and absorptive capacity, are provided for. Finally, the model allows for the analysis of movements of energy and funds among regions and the effects of such flows on the economies and balance of payments of those areas. All the above problems and relationships are dealt with simultaneously on a regional basis and under consistent and similar assumptions. The utilization of such a comprehensive framework avoids piecemeal and isolated analysis of the integrated and complex world energy markets. It is the framework and model themselves which are important, however, rather than the results generated under the particular set of assumptions used. Under more pessimistic or optimistic sets of assumptions, the model will generate different results.

The world energy model is a synthesis of the most advanced approaches developed by the author and many other individuals to analyze energy problems. This book also has substantial value to nonquantitative analytical policy makers and students in the energy field, since it conceptualizes the interaction of the various components of the world energy markets and makes the interaction of cost, price, supply, demand, and technology variables easily traceable.

The results presented in this book should be considered preliminary. Only time and extensive use of the model in simulating policy-making processes and further upgrading of the data and modeling structure will prove the usefulness of such a comprehensive approach toward energy modeling and analysis of world energy-related issues.

The next chapter presents an overview of the world energy economy followed by a chapter describing a framework for analyzing that economy. Parts II and III of the book present a world energy model, which is constructed on the basis of the framework presented in Part I. Part II presents energy demand and supply models for the oil-importing countries. Part III deals with oil supply models of the OPEC member countries and analyzes their price and production strategies. Part IV sums up the book by presenting a summary, conclusions, and implications for future energy modeling research.

2

Major Participants in the World Energy Economy

This chapter presents a general picture of the actual world energy economy and the way in which its various participants interact. Technical terms and quantitative exposition are avoided in order to facilitate general understanding of the overall operation of the world energy markets, including the price, production, and consumption decision processes of all the participants involved.

Countries are not equally endowed with energy resources. Major industrial countries consume most of the energy produced, and because of the inadequacy of their indigenous energy resources, they are also major energy importers. These countries are mostly members of the Organization for Economic Cooperation and Development (OECD).[1] The members of the Organization for Petroleum Exporting Countries (OPEC), on the other hand, are endowed with large amounts of petroleum and natural gas resources but consume only small quantities. They are major petroleum exporters. At present, coal does not constitute a major portion of international energy transactions. It is quite likely, however, that with growing costs of alternative energy resources, coal may also play an important future role in international energy movements. Generally, international trade in energy is an indispensible part of the operations of the economies of all countries.

International energy transactions are the net result of complex decision processes among the participants in the world energy markets. The major groups of participants are as follows: (1) consumers, producers, and governments of oil-importing countries;[2] (2) the international energy companies which operate in various phases of energy markets in both oil-importing and oil-exporting countries; and (3) the governments of oil-exporting countries.[3] Continuous cooperation of the participants in the world energy market is essential in order to ensure an uninterrupted supply of oil to the consuming countries and a resultant flow of earnings to the oil-producing countries and to the international energy companies. Basically, this cooperation is determined by the amount of benefit that each participant obtains for its contribution. If the actual reward does not match the desired return, conflict will arise. In order to remove conflict, a balance must be achieved between many essential political, social, and commercial variables. Hopefully, the net result would be a stable equilibrium for all elements of the world energy markets.

7

The functional markets in which the participants interact are production, transportation, refining and conversion, and distribution. The primary energy and final products involved are crude oil, natural gas, coal, uranium, oil shale, petroleum products, and electricity.

Price is both a major determinant of international energy transactions and the net result of the interaction of supply and demand for alternative energy forms in various geographic regions. Supply and demand are dependent upon the availability of reserves, life-style of consumers, degree of industrialization, availability of alternative fuels, rate of economic growth, and availability of new energy technology and capital, as well as many other factors. The participants in the international energy markets control or influence the factors which influence supply and demand for various energy forms and therefore influence energy prices.

The relative strength of the participants in controlling the above-mentioned factors varies. The controlling forces in the first group of participants, the oil-importing countries, are consumers, producers, and governments in these countries. Consumers and governments control energy demand through conservation and energy efficiency measures, tariffs and taxes, environmental programs, fuel switching, and other measures. Producers and governments control energy supply and production through new energy research and development, tax incentives, investment programs, price regulations, developing alternative energy resources and recovery techniques, changes in environmental restrictions, and energy pacts among oil-importing countries (e.g., International Energy Agency).

The second group of participants, the international energy companies, has strong control over domestic and international activities in the areas of production, transportation, refining, and distribution of energy products. Further, they have overwhelming capability in management, know-how, and financing of energy-related activities. Thus, their influence over pricing, supply, and distribution is quite normal.

The third group of participants, the oil-exporting countries (OPEC), has overwhelming control and influence in world pricing, production, and investment policies. They control the major world reserves of crude oil and natural gas. Their large surplus oil revenues are being used to penetrate international transportation, refining, and distribution activity.

The interaction of these participants in world energy markets determines the final equilibrium price, supply, demand, imports, and exports of all energy forms in each geographic region. Further, they also determine the activity levels of such operations as transportation and refining.

World energy markets cannot be identified with a single theoretical market structure, such as perfect competition, "oilgopoly," monopoly, regulated, etc. They are too complex for a single classification. This complexity makes an equilbrium determination of prices, supply, and demand more difficult. In each of the world energy markets, one or more characteristics of some of the market structures may be identified. For instance, OPEC should be considered a cartel (oligopoly) rather than a monopoly because of the lack of cohesion among its members. However, even the cartel classification should be qualified because of the existence of barter arrangements between some OPEC members and oil-importing countries. On the other hand, a greater degree of competition exists in the refining and distribution markets of the oil-importing countries. Thus, the world energy economy is constituted of numerous markets with different levels of competition, and it is within these markets that equilibrium price, supply, and demand are determined.

The remainder of this chapter describes how decisions made by any of the participants in energy markets affect the decisions of other participants.

Consumers in oil-importing countries are major decision makers in final energy end-use markets (industrial, commercial, residential, and transportation). They allocate a certain portion of their income among alternative final energy products based on both the relative prices of fuels and the Btu content, burning efficiency, and ease of handling and storage of those fuels. An increase in the relative price of any one fuel may lead to increases in the demand for the other (substitute) fuels and increased energy conservation of the initial fuel.

Governments of oil-importing countries influence consumers' demand for alternative energy forms by enacting environmental regulations, conservation programs, and tax measures. Consumer reaction to changes in relative prices and to the various measures varies for each final product, within each demand sector, and for each year and geographic region.

Producers and governments of the oil-importing countries control or influence the supply and availability of indigenous energy sources. Producers do so through their capital investment decisions, which affect new energy reserve discoveries, production, and new energy technology and recovery techniques. These producers' decisions are influenced by the relative costs and prices of all forms of energy. Governments of oil-importing countries also influence the supply and production of indigenous resources through their energy research and development programs, leasing policies, tax measures, environmental programs, regulation of activities of energy industries, etc. Producers' reactions to changes in relative costs and prices and to the various policies and measures vary for each primary form of energy, for each year, and for each geographic region.

In most cases, primary energy forms are transported, refined, and converted to final energy forms and distributed for use by consumers. Some of these activities are performed within a region under the control and influence of domestic producers, distributors, and governments of the oil-importing countries. Many of the domestic producers and distributors are international energy companies which have integrated energy operations throughout the world.

The domestic consumers, producers, and governments of the oil-importing countries interact with one another. Each attempts to exercise control and influence the market to its advantage in order to achieve its goals. Some of the elements of control were discussed above. Most of the energy demand of oil-importing countries cannot be satisfied with indigenous energy sources. The remaining demand, when not curtailed by government action, is satisfied by imported foreign energy resources. The level of this demand for each country or region varies at different price levels. The governments in the oil-importing countries substantially affect the demand for energy imports. Various measures, such as tariffs, quotas, etc., are introduced by these governments in the name of national security, balance-of-payments, protection of domestic energy industry, etc. The demand for energy imports, for example, is a by-product of a complex interaction, control, influence, and decisions by consumers, producers, and governments of the oil-importing countries. The level of oil-importing countries' demand for OPEC oil plays a central role in the decisions and reactions of the oil-exporting countries.

The price and production strategies of the oil-exporting countries (OPEC) are significantly influenced by demand for their oil. There is no guarantee that OPEC will collectively satisfy this demand at a set price. OPEC price and production strategies are also heavily influenced by the decisions of individual members because of the lack of perfect cohesiveness among them. Their decisions are influenced by their relative capacity to absorb oil revenues, their different economic infrastructures, the relative size of oil reserves and production, differences in population, relative availability of nonenergy resources, etc. OPEC's price, production, and investment decisions will subsequently influence the world economy as a whole, as well as their own ability to remain as a cartel.

This chapter presented a brief overview of the operation of real world energy forces and markets. A comprehensive analytical framework is required in order to measure the degree of control and influence of the participants in the world energy economy on one another. The next chapter presents such a framework.

3

A Framework for Analyzing the World Energy Economy

The emergence of the so-called energy crisis has forced many countries, particularly the industrialized nations, to assess their present energy positions and to plan the development of their energy resources. The crisis has led to Project Independence in the United States, to similar programs in other countries, and to formation of the International Energy Agency to coordinate some of these energy programs. These energy plans were devised in light of the world energy market and, in particular, around likely future OPEC petroleum price and production strategies. In other words, expected future OPEC petroleum prices and production determine the economic attractiveness of developing alternative energy resources. Of course, this is only one side of the issue. Availability of domestic energy resources and access to commercially proved technology are among the many factors which determine the success of any plan for developing national energy resources and the probability of attaining "independence" from foreign energy sources.

Energy analysis and planning are complicated by the inherent complexity of the energy sector as well as by its interaction with domestic and foreign economies. Thus, construction of an analytical framework for use as a planning tool is indispensible. Such a framework should have a number of characteristics. First, the framework should be oriented to international policy, since such a large share of world oil is traded internationally. Second, it should view the energy problem within an integrated equilibrium environment consisting of energy supply, transportation, distribution, and consumption. Third, it should provide for interfuel competition in analyzing the demand for alternative energy products in different end-use markets based on prices, as well as provide for interresource substitution for analyzing the development of alternative resources based upon resource costs and technology in exploration, development, transportation, processing, electric generation, and other sectors. Fourth, the framework should provide for interaction between energy and nonenergy sectors of the economy. Fifth, the framework should incorporate the interaction between OPEC member countries, oil-importing countries, and international oil companies.[1]

This chapter presents a framework that subsequently will be used to analyze the world energy economy. Most of the elements of the framework presented in this chapter are used in subsequent chapters to construct a world energy model. That model and its application constitute the core of this book.

The framework for analysis of the world energy economy has the above-mentioned characteristics and is divided into two major parts. The first deals with interfuel competition for analyzing demand and inter-resource substitution for analyzing supply of various energy forms in the oil-importing countries. More specifically, it specifies the variables and relationships underlying demand, supply, prices, and flows of various energy forms in oil-importing countries. The second part deals with the interaction of the oil-exporting countries (OPEC) with the oil-importing countries. It describes the variables and relationships underlying the oil-exporting countries' price, production, and investment decisions. It also deals with the stability and capacity of these countries to absorb oil reve-nues and the availability of petrodollars for recycling to the industrial countries. The role of the international oil companies in bringing together the above two participants is explained.

A schematic presentation of the entire framework is presented in Figure 3-1 to which the reader is referred throughout this chapter. The first two pages of the figure show the major areas of demand and supply in the oil-importing countries, which are discussed in the next section. The sec-ond two pages show the interaction between the oil-exporting and oil-importing countries, which is discussed in the final section of this chapter. The arrows in the figure reflect the direction of effect between the two parts and the interaction between the framework as well as among the sectors within each part.

Energy Demand and Supply in the Oil-Importing Countries

This part of the framework deals with the interaction of energy supply and demand in the oil-importing countries and the factors which influence them, as shown in the first two pages of Figure 3-1.

The demand for alternative final energy products is a function of its own price and of those of competing fuels in a particular end-use market[2] of an oil-importing country. Further, this demand depends on the level of domes-tic economic activity. The supply of alternative primary energy forms is a function of costs and availabilities of energy resources in each oil-importing country. The technology of exploration, production, transportation, refin-ing, and other energy conversion processes also affects the supply of primary energy resources.

The supply and demand for each energy form for each end-use market in a country and the supply and demand for related technologies are treated simultaneously to arrive at equilibrium prices and quantities. That is, energy resources are made available at their respective locations, transported to desired destinations, and refined or otherwise transformed to meet price sensitive end-product energy demand.[3]

The simultaneous determination of equilibrium energy demands, supplies, and prices for different regions[4] of the world within this part of the framework makes it possible to answer the following questions which are frequently raised by policy makers in both OPEC and the oil-importing countries.

1. What are the likely world equilibrium prices, supply, demand, imports, and flows of alternative energy forms under different scenarios?
2. How much refining, electricity generation, production, and transportation capacities and investments are required to meet the forecasted energy demand?
3. What is the demand for OPEC oil by oil-importing countries at different price levels?
4. How dependent will particular consuming countries be on oil-exporting countries?
5. What will be the impact of environmental restrictions, conservation measures, and introduction of new energy technology on world energy supply-and-demand balances and prices?

Interfuel Competition and Energy Demand Analysis

Analysis of interfuel competition is the nucleus for forecasting demand and market shares of competing forms of energy in various end-use markets. The degree of interfuel competition can be most effectively measured at the lowest possible level of aggregation; i.e., country analysis is superior to regional analysis. Aggregate analysis combines nonhomogeneous data and dampens all the major variations in behavior existing at the country level. These variations stem from differences between countries in income, degree of industrialization, prices of fuels, distance from the fuel source, population, etc. Further, competition among fuels for meeting energy demand varies among different end-use markets in a country, and the intensity of such competition differs among countries.

The following subsections describe interfuel competition and energy demand in the major end-use markets.

Interaction of Inter-Fuel Competition and Inter-Resource Substitution in the Oil Importing Countries

Econometric representation of inter-fuel competition (demand)   Interaction of energy supply and demand (equilibrium analysis)

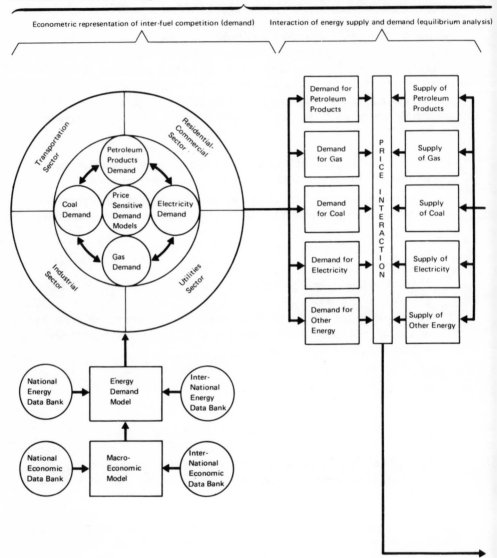

Figure 3-1. An Analytical Framework for World Energy Markets.

Econometric-Linear Programming Representation of Inter-Resource Substitution (Supply)

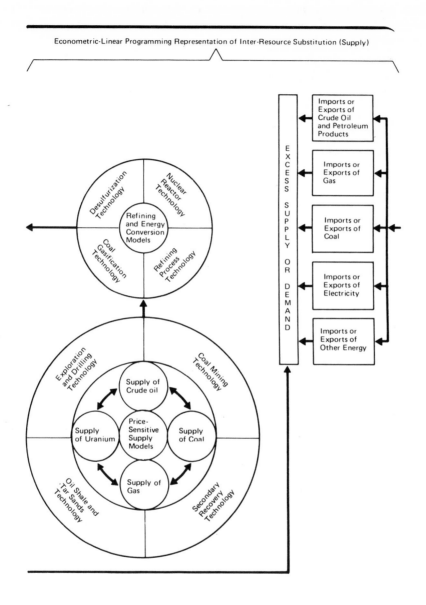

Interaction of the Oil Exporting Countries with the Oil Importing Countries

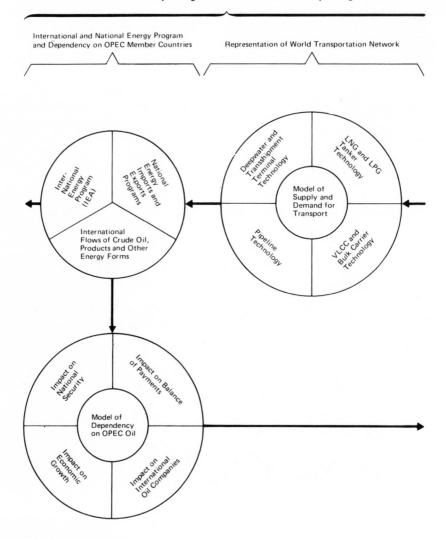

Figure 3-1 (Continued)

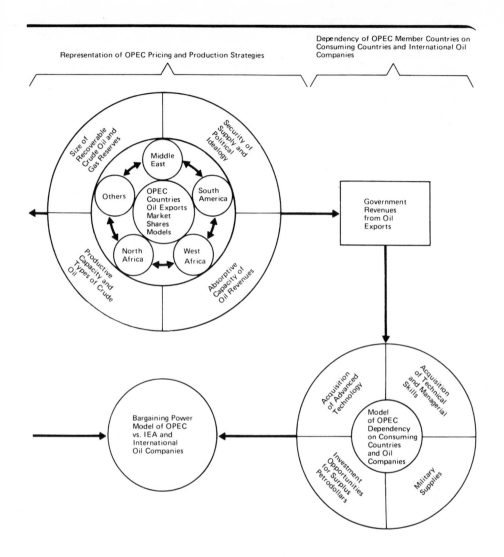

Demand in the Transportation Sector. There is virtually no interfuel competition among alternative forms of energy to meet the demand of the transportation sector. Petroleum products dominate this market. Each product is used in a specialized type of engine and carrier. Motor vehicles, aircraft, railroads, farm vehicles, and water carriers use gasoline, aviation fuel, jet fuel, diesel fuel, or bunker fuel oil. The demand for gasoline is basically dependent upon the stock of motor vehicles, long-term prices of gasoline, average miles driven per vehicle, and average miles per gallon. The stock of motor vehicles is in turn dependent upon the number of households, incomes of households, multiple-car ownership, demographic factors, alternative transportation systems, central-city congestion, and other factors.

Jet fuel, like gasoline, has a specialized market and does not face any competition from alternative fuels. The demand for jet fuel is a function of the demand for air travel. Population, airfare, leisure time, education, disposable income, and level of business activity determine the level of demand for air transportation and, consequently, for jet fuel.

The demand for diesel fuel is another considerable component of energy demand in the transportation sector. The demand for diesel fuel can be expressed as a function of the number of diesel cars, buses, trucks, railroads, and farm vehicles. The demand for bunker fuel is basically restricted to marine transportation.

Total energy demand in the transportation sector is equal to the summation of all the demand components mentioned above.

Demand in the Residential-Commercial Sector. Interfuel competition for satisfying the demand for energy in the residential-commercial end-use market is intense. The demand for energy in this sector is the sum of the demand in space heating, water heating, air conditioning, cooking, refrigeration, lighting, and so forth. Distillate fuel oil, coal, gas, and electricity compete in space heating; gas and electricity compete in cooking and air conditioning; and electricity is a sole energy source for lighting.

Distillate fuel and coal are less attractive as home-heating fuel than are electric heat and natural gas.[5] However, distillate fuel oil and coal are still the principal home-heating fuels used in areas where there are inadequate supplies of natural gas or in areas with limited electric energy. Distillate fuel oil and coal suffer from being not as clean, convenient, or trouble-free as gas or electricity, and oil burner equipment is inherently more expensive than gas burner equipment.

The growth of natural gas in space heating is mostly due to its attractive price with respect to alternative fuels, cleanliness, continuous availability without need for storage, supply dependability, efficiency of utilization, and low prices of natural-gas space heating equipment. On the other hand, the inadequacy of gas supplies in many regions is quite apparent. Because of transportation costs, gas is a relatively high-cost energy source in areas distant from gas-producing areas. In the past, the price of natural gas was relatively lower than prices of coal and fuel oil because of the over abundance of gas reserves, price stability through long-term contracts, and regulatory restrictions.

Electricity began competing with distillate fuel oil, coal, and natural gas in the space heating market only about a decade ago. During this short period, its use has grown rapidly, especially in new homes. Electric heat does not require any piping or storage space, and it is clean. The growing popularity of air conditioning not only is expanding electricity consumption in its own right but also is aiding the spread of electric heat. There is little doubt that consumption of electricity for space heating is presently relatively expensive and also entails additional construction and insulation expense. The use of electricity for cooking and electrical appliances is also growing.

The price and supply of alternative home-heating fuels are more likely to determine the space heating mode than anything else. Furthermore, incomes of households, number of appliances, degree of urbanization, and several other factors influence the choice of the household among competing fuels as well as determine the level of energy demanded by the residential-commercial sector.

Demand for natural gas, oil, and electricity basically has the same determinants. The demand for distillate fuel oil is a function of its price, prices of natural gas and electricity, stock of oil burners in use, number of households, average degree days, personal income, and other factors. Similarly, the demand for natural gas and electricity is a function of their prices, of the prices of competing fuels, and of the other variables mentioned above.

The total demand for energy in this sector can be derived by summing the demand for distillate fuel oil, natural gas, electricity, and other fuels such as coal.

Demand in the Industrial Sector. The industrial sector uses energy in various forms. Unlike in the other sectors, most of the energy is used to produce products for other than final use. For instance, coaking coal is used for steel making, electricity is used for making aluminum, and so forth. Many forms of energy, including LPG, natural gas, coal, residual fuel oil, etc., are used in varying degrees in the industrial sector. For some applications, one type of energy form dominates without significant competition from other fuels; in other applications, competition is more intense. As a result of the diversity in industrial processes and varying intensities of energy use, the industrial sector should be divided into major industry subgroups, such as steel, aluminum, plastic, glass, cement, paper, rubber, and food processing. The major determinant of energy demand in the industrial sector is the level of industrial production. The industrial use of electric power has increased rapidly; in recent years, consumption has increased at a rate in excess of the rate of increase in industrial production.

The price of energy is also of major importance for a cost-conscious and competitive industry. Higher prices for energy lead to improved process efficiency, heat management, conservation practices, and eventual reduction in energy consumption in relation to other inputs. Further, technological change also can reduce the energy requirements in the industrial sectors. However, in less energy-intensive industries, the rise in energy costs may not generate enough incentives to adopt new capital-intensive, energy-conserving processes. Thus, the impact of higher prices on demand for energy in the industrial sector is related to the ratio of the cost of energy inputs to the total cost of the product, as well as to the type of industry.

Demand in the Electric Utility Sector. Total demand for electricity is the sum of electricity consumed in the residential-commercial, transportation, and industrial sectors. Electric utilities, therefore, cannot be classified as end-users of energy, except to the trivial extent that they use energy to light and heat their own plants. Thus, for more effective presentation, the electric utility sector is presented on the supply side. In other words, the choice of electric utilities among fuels such as coal, oil, natural gas, or nuclear is treated as an "interresource substitution" process rather than as a component in "interfuel competition" in the end-use markets. This discussion is presented later in this chapter.

Interresource Substitution and Energy Supply Analysis

The demand levels and market shares for alternative fuels in each end-use market are determined through the process of interfuel competition, as described in the preceding section. The next step is to consider factors which affect the supply of energy resources. The primary forms of energy supplied are coal, oil, gas, uranium (nuclear), and oil shale. A high degree of interresource substitution exists among these sources of supply. Available and prospective technology in the areas of desulfurization, coal gasification and liquefaction, synthetic fuel from shale, nuclear reactors, offshore exploration, secondary recovery, etc., contribute greatly to this substitution. Costs and the level of technology are two major determinants of supply capacity.

The following sections describe interresource substitution in analyzing the supply of crude oil, natural gas, electric power, and coal.

Crude Oil and Natural Gas Supply. The challenge facing the oil and gas industry is not that of finding substantial volumes of petroleum reserves, but that of finding reserves which are recoverable at a reasonable cost. Thus, cost will be a determining factor in the supply availability and the relative shares of production of various energy forms.

The following factors have been cited as causes of the historical decline in exploration and development of oil and gas in the United States: (1) a long-term decline in the real price of domestic crude oil, (2) the federal administration of well-head prices of interstate gas sales at levels too low to attract investment, (3) too high a tax burden on oil and gas producers, (4) uncertainties about oil import programs, and (5) increasing costs and difficulties experienced by the industry in finding new oil and gas reservoirs. Environmtal considerations have further delayed discoveries of crude oil reserves and have impeded the expansion of producing capacity. Alaskan North Slope production and offshore leasing have been delayed for this reason. A rise in the rate of exploration and development of new oil and gas in the United States that is adequate to keep pace with the anticipated growth in demand can be attained by higher real prices and improved cost-reducing technology. However, higher real prices for petroleum are unlikely to provide the right answers for balancing demand and supply for several reasons. First, price increases sufficient to bring forth enough new supply would depress growth in demand below the level anticipated. Second, price increases would stimulate efforts to develop higher-cost substitutes for crude oil and natural gas from coal and shale. Third, they would increase the price of crude oil produced by oil-exporting countries relative to the price of OPEC oil and thereby induce additional importation or encourage the development of other domestic resources of energy by oil-importing countries including nuclear power. Technological advances offer the best alternative to the domestic industry in providing increased supplies of oil and gas at reasonable prices. Technological developments will reduce exploration and development costs and improve recovery.

Long-term domestic crude oil and natural gas supplies (and capacity) can be estimated as a function of costs and prices. (In other words, supply and capacity can be estimated as a function of profit per barrel of crude and per thousand cubic feet of natural gas.[6])

Discoveries of new crude oil and natural gas reserves are the product of exploration and development efforts. The new reserve discoveries of crude oil and natural gas are dependent upon the number of wildcats drilled, the success ratio, the average size of discovery per successful wildcat, and the growth in secondary recovery technology.

One of the determinants of annual drilling is the profit or expected profit from drilling versus the expected profit from alternative investment projects. For instance, if the profit margin on secondary recovery efforts exceeds the profit margin on drilling, a larger share of the available funds will be allocated to recovery. Thus, all the major factors which influence returns and costs should be taken into account in determining the number of wildcats to be drilled. The expected wel-head prices of crude oil and natural gas are of major importance. Expected government subsidies and tax laws will also influence expected profit and drilling decisions. The cost per barrel of crude oil and per thousand cubic feet of natural gas and their present value are of significance in determining the number of wildcats drilled. The previous success ratio also will influence the decision to drill.[7]

Coal Supply. Coal is the main fuel for electric power generation. Historically, the tonnage used for this purpose has increased over time, but its share has decreased. Continued imporvements in mining, transportation, and utilization technologies have kept coal prices competitive with other fossil fuels in areas close to coal fields. These technological advances have partially offset increased production costs, including higher costs of health, safety, and environmental regulations. Technologies which may increase coal's future competitiveness in the interresource substitution process are stack gas desulfurization, coal liquefaction and gasification, and more efficient mining technology.

Coal presents not only the greatest number but also the most complex problems among the primary energy resources. In the United States, for example, coal resources are currently estimated to be about 3210 billion tons. About one-half of these resources may be recoverable. Approximately two-thirds of total resources are west of the Mississippi River, but 90 percent of the coal produced is burned east of it, with the electric power industry consuming more than one-half of the total national output. Many of these resources have such a high sulfur content that they cannot be sold under existing emission regulations. Further, although there exist large reserves of high-quality coal suitable for strip mining, this technique has been a prime target of objection on the part of ecologists and legislators.

A potentially great market for coal is in liquefaction and gasification. Despite certain advantages of coal over other synthetic fuel sources, there are major obstacles in converting coal to synthetic hydrocarbons: the massive inputs of hydrogen and water needed, the large investment risks involved in the construction of necessarily large plant units, and the need for tremendous volumes of coal at a single plant.

In the past, coal mines could be opened with comparatively little investment because the principal ingredient was labor rather than expensive equipment. Gradually, the coal mines mechanized, the number of laborers was reduced, and productivity increased.

Coal, which has been the dominant fuel for generating electricity for many years, is faced with the following constraints in the United States and, to some degree, in other countries.

1. A shortage of miners for underground mines as it becomes increasingly difficult to attract young people into the coal industry
2. Difficulties arising from strict coal mine health and safety laws
3. Air pollution and water pollution control requirements beyond the reach of current technology
4. Severe restrictions on strip mining
5. A shortage of low-sulfur coal (less than 1 percent sulfur)
6. Inability of some utilities to get long-term coal contracts
7. The increased cost of mining coal resulting from increases in the prices of equipment, material, services, and transportation

New air pollution developments concerning sulfur dioxide have threatened the coal industry's future. Several sulfur-removal systems have been developed recently. However, at present, the cost of these sulfur-removal operations cannot be reliably estimated.

Three types of supply horizons can be associated with coal: short, medium, and long term. The responsiveness of coal supply to changes in price is quite sensitive to the time span within which the incremental tonnage is to be produced. Short-term (1 year) coal supply seems to be quite insensitive, while long-term coal supply (5 to 20 years) seems quite sensitive to changes in price.

A number of factors limit the incremental amount of coal which can be produced and made available for consumption within the short-term time frame. New mines capable of producing significant tonnages cannot be developed and brought into production within a year. The only new capacity which can come onstream during the year is from mines which had been previously planned in order to replace the tonnage lost from mines depleted during the year and to provide for the expected growth in demand. Beyond this, any incremental supply comes from existing mines by increasing production to full capacity.

In the intermediate term, established mining companies could bring new mines which were planned during the first year into production by the third to fifth year. However, it is not likely that new firms could enter the industry and develop a significant productive capacity within this time span. Growth in supply would still have to come from the existing industry during this period of time.

The long-term supply period covers a time span during which existing firms can develop new coal mines or deplete old ones and during which new firms can enter the industry and old ones can leave. There are a number of factors that could affect the long-term supply of coal. Either these factors could limit the industry's capacity for growth, or they could affect the cost of producing coal at various growth rates or with time. These factors are: (1) labor supply, (2) availability of an adequate transportation system, (3) trends in the cost of capital equipment and operating supplies, (4) trends in technology, (5) government policies, (6) adequate coal reserves, and (7) the industry's ability to generate the capital required for growth.

Electric Power Supply. Electricity is generated in fossil fuel, nuclear, and hydroelectric plants. Most of the electric utility power plants are of the fossil fuel type and burn coal, residual fuel oil, distillate, or natural gas. In many cases, a certain degree of flexibility exists for utilities to convert from one fuel to another. This interresource substitution reflects present and future relative fuel prices, the relative availability of fuels, environmental constraints, and proximity to sources of fuel supply.

Coal has been the dominant fuel in the steam electric generating industry during the past decade. Recent advances in mining technology and coal hauling will help it to maintain this position. In the past decade, there was a growing demand for oil-fired power plants despite the development of nuclear power plants. Oil-powered stations were being built because of the increasing cost of coal and the long period of time and the high cost required to build nuclear power plants. Additionally, utilities were having trouble finding appropriate sites for nuclear plants because of possible radioactive pollution. However, coal-fired power plants have become considerably more attractive in recent years because of the large increase in oil prices.

The main justification for nuclear power or any fuel for the electric utility industry is economics, although there are other factors such as the limited supply of fossil fuels, prevention of air and water pollution, etc. There is some proof that nuclear power costs less in most areas. However, large-scale nuclear units may not be preferable in all situations. Further, nuclear units rarely will be purchased for peak shaving under present technology. Finally, other considerations such as mine-mouth plant situations, additions to existing stations, and low-capital cost units for fast start-up service may favor fossil fuels. Also, future nuclear units will have to compete with a constantly improving fossil fuel technology. On the other hand, growing public concern over air pollution from fossil fuel units may dictate either the use of more expensive, low-sulfur fuels or the addition of sulfur-removal facilities.

One of the most important long-term considerations in the nuclear field is the cost and availability of the fuel itself. As with a fossil fuel plant, fuel costs over the life of a nuclear station will total substantially more than the cost of the plant itself. The cost of nuclear fuel includes charges for raw uranium oxide, conversion, enrichment, fabrication, and reprocessing, reduced by credits for depleted uranium, plutonium, and other by-product recoveries.

In recent years, nuclear power programs have been set back seriously because of high costs, long lead times, fears of nuclear contamination, and hardware failures. Soaring costs and construction delays have led to a few nuclear power plant cancellations, and in some cases utilities are ordering fossil fuel plants instead.

Electric generation capacity requirements are a function of demand for electricity, as well as of the prices and availability of alternative fuels, labor, and power plant equipment. Electric generation capacity is further affected by reserve requirements and load (peak, intermediate, and base) variation, capacity factors, and transmission losses. Nuclear power plants, large high-efficiency coal or oil-fired steam turbine plants, or hydroelectric plants usually are used to satisfy base-load electricity requirements. To satisfy peak-load demand, pumped storage hydroelectric, gas, or diesel turbines are used. Since peak-load plants operate only a small part of the time, fuel costs are less important and the primary objective is to minimize the investment cost while obtaining reliable quick-start and shutdown capability.

More than 40 percent of electricity generation capacity remains under-utilized because of daily and seasonal fluctuations in demand for electricity. Further, combustion inefficiency and transmission losses of electricity account for more than 60 percent of energy consumed at the utilities. Higher prices for coal, oil, natural gas, and nuclear power will lead to better load management, reduction in overall electricity usage in the end-use market, and improvement in conversion and transmission efficiencies.

Nuclear generation capacity installed can be forecasted as a function of relevant variables. The difference between total installed electric capacity, which is estimated based on the total demand for electricity, and nuclear capacity installed will represent fossil fuel plant capacity requirements. Then the market share of utility power plants burning oil, coal, and gas can be determined based on the underlying variables.

Price Determination for Alternative Energy Forms

Once the supply and demand for alternative energy forms in the oil-importing countries are determined, equilibrium prices can be estimated. The first two pages of Figure 3-1 show graphically how equilibrium prices are determined through interfuel competition on the demand side and interresource substitution on the supply side. This section describes some of the important factors which influence the prices of alternative energy forms.

Prices of primary energy and petroleum products play a dominant role in determining demand and supply of alternative forms of energy. Price elasticities of demand for alternative forms of energy affect pricing decisions. These elasticities can be categorized into short-run and long-run and by end-use market, such as residential-commercial, utilities, or industrial demand.

The distinction between short and long-run price elasticities is important. A reduction in the price of one fuel is likely to have an immediate as well as a long-run effect, and consumers will adjust their demand to the new price. Of course, before the final or long-run adjustment is completed, there will be some time lag during which consumers will respond partially to the new price. Therefore it is likely that a reduction in price maynot lead to an immediate pronounced increase in demand, but that it will do so as time passes.

In the long run, the demand and supply of almost all fuels is price-elastic—even the demand for gasoline, which faces minimal competition from other fuels. In residential-commercial, industrial, and utilities sectors where the degree of interfuel competition is severe, not only the price of each fuel but also the prices of competing fuels play an important role in determining the market shares and demand for alternative fuels.

The demand and market share for any commodity will usually be positively related to the prices of its substitutes and to household income. For instance, this relationship holds for distillate fuel, natural gas, and electricity in the residential-commercial market. But distillate fuel may be treated as an inferior good in areas with higher levels of household income, warmer climate, and abundant supplies of the substitute good—natural gas. Even if the price of the inferior distillate good goes down, the demand and market share for it may decrease; and as the income of the household increases, there may be a substitution of superior fuels such as natural gas or electricity for the inferior good. Thus, in addition to the fuel's own price elasticity, the cross elasticities of competing fuels are important for analysis.

Determinants of Crude Oil and Product Prices. The prices of crude oil and petroleum products in the oil-importing countries are highly correlated with the prices of imported crude oil from OPEC member countries. Frequently, domestic petroleum prices are brought up to par with imported petroleum prices by governments of the oil-importing countries in order to discourage large amounts of crude oil imports and to encourage expansion of domestic crude oil production. Measures adopted by governments to maintain domestic prices at par with imported prices are higher petroleum-product taxes, deregulation of regulated prices of certain petroleum products or natural gas, imposition of tariffs, or simply allowing higher margins for oil companies. Thus, one of the major determinants of domestic petroleum prices is the price of OPEC oil.

Future prices of imported crude oil, natural gas, and liquefied natural gas from OPEC member countries will probably depend upon OPEC's oil revenue requirements, the degree of participation, production policies, and price escalation clauses built into concession agreements. OPEC member countries have expressed increasing interest in linking crude and hydro-carbon prices to various price indices for industrial products in the importing countries in order to protect their prices against future price uncertainties resulting from inflation, exchange rate fluctuations, and price increases for imported commodities. Among the price indices proposed are the wholesale price index, the cost of living index, price indices of industrial products most frequently exported to OPEC member countries, and the average fuel price index of competing fuels.

The above hypothesis concerning the determinants of future OPEC energy prices may be valid if intercountry competition among OPEC members to obtain a greater petroleum export share does not accelerate and if OPEC members retain their unified price and production policy goals. Some countries now constrain their production to conserve reserves in order to gain the advantage of higher future prices. Others are expanding their production in order to finance domestic development projects. To the extent that restriction and expansion of crude oil production offset each other, prices will not decline. However, if competition among OPEC member countries for higher petroleum export shares becomes severe, a decline in crude oil prices is inevitable.

Prices of imported natural gas from OPEC countries will probably be related to imported crude oil prices, adjusted for the quality superiority of natural gas.

Prices of jointly produced petroleum products are mainly a function of production costs. Prices of these products are therefore quite dependent on one another. Even though each product has its own peculiar supply/demand characteristics which are likely to create a different price behavior, the supply of each product is at least in part the result of the demand for related products, and the demand conditions for each such product appear to vary considerably from one product to another.

An examination of historical price relationships among certain jointly produced petroleum products (gasoline, kerosene, distillate fuel oil, and diesel fuel) for the past two decades provides several interesting observations. First, major price changes for these different products coincide with one another. This may be due to the fact that making more of one product means making less of another. It appears that oil companies most often use cost rather than demand as a basis for price setting. That is not to say that demand is unimportant. For example, it is an important price determinant for distillate fuel and residual fuel oil, which face severe competition from coal, natural gas, electricity, and nuclear energy. Also, diesel fuel and No.

2 heating oil have a high degree of physical similarity and probably cost about the same to make, but the markets for the two products are dissimilar and an entirely different price behavior prevails in these markets. Nevertheless, there is limited competition among petroleum products even though there is competition between different forms of energy.

A further complication in explaining prices of petroleum products is the relationship of such prices to prices for crude oil. Do crude oil prices depend on product prices or vice versa? In the past, crude oil prices have not changed as frequently and to as great an extent as have product prices, even though the patterns of movements have been similar. The determinants of particular petroleum product prices are considered below.

The price of gasoline is basically determined by factors influencing supply rather than demand. In the short run, changes in gasoline stocks are a major determinant, but in the long run the degree of capacity utilization is more important. Other important factors are the cost of crude, the cost of producing gasoline, and the preceding year's demand and prices. Further, an increase in production of distillate may lead to an increase in the production of gasoline and to a reduction in gasoline prices.

The cost of producing gasoline is difficult to measure because it involves a joint production of many refined products including kerosene, jet fuel, distillate, and residual fuel oil. Further, refiners have the capability of maximizing profits by changing petroleum product yield patterns. Thus, the pricing of gasoline or other products depends upon average costs and revenues for all products, stocks of refined products, and capacity utilization of the processes used for making a particular product.

Historical analysis shows that gasoline and heating oil prices have been relatively higher and residual fuel oil relatively lower than crude oil prices. This relationship results from use of the joint product pricing method, in which the average price of all petroleum products rather than the price of an individual product is significant. The lower price level for residual fuel compared to that for other petroleum products is due to the fact that residual fuel oil meets relatively greater competition from other forms of energy such as coal, gas, and nuclear energy in the utilities and industrial markets.

The price of fuel oil (distillate or residual) is a function of the average revenue from a unit of refined product. The theory of optimum product mix and least-cost combination of inputs provides only a partial guide to explaining the relationship of fuel oil prices to the average realization from all products. Theoretically, marginal revenue ratios for specified products should be equal to the ratios of their marginal costs. Further, a close parallel exists between the marginal revenue and the price of a particular product. This does not, however, ensure that the price of a particular product will have a stable relationship with that of another refined product. As the consumption mix changes, the product mix is changed, marginal cost ratios change, and marginal revenue ratios will likewise change. Fuel oil prices are highly correlated with the average cost of refined products. Further, empirical observation shows that the average realization for all products is highly correlated with their average cost.

Petroleum refiners change the yields of various petroleum products based on the market prices and production costs for those products. For example, the introduction of new cracking technology in the United States during the past two decades has led to a reduction in refinery yields of residual fuel oil. However, the situation is almost the opposite in Europe and Japan. Further, future prices for residual fuel oil in the United States are highly uncertain because of the by-product nature of residual fuel oil production and its declining yield, increased air pollution restrictions, the declining demand for high-sulfur fuel, and uncertain future prices for imported crude oil.

Determinants of Coal Prices. The price of coal at the mine depends on the cost of labor, capital, and other operating costs such as maintenance and power. To these costs must be added the cost of improving mine safety and environmental costs, such as land reclamation. Labor and capital productivity and the thickness of coal seams also affect costs and prices.

Most coal is consumed in utility power plants and in industrial operations. Transportation costs therefore also affect price. The as-burned cost of coal per ton to these power plants is equal to the average price of coal per ton f.o.b. mine plus the average rail (or other modes of transportation) freight charge per ton. The average rail freight charge is a function of the average capacity of freight cars, daily mileage of freight cars, and several other variables. A reasonable rate of return on investment should be added to production cost to ensure continuing expansion of coal production capacity. In general, the as-burned cost or price for alternative fuels (coal, residual fuel, and gas) to utilities and industrial users is the most meaningful criterion for selecting among competing fuels.

International Energy Flows and Transportation

The preceding sections of this chapter dealt with supply, demand, and price interaction among alternative energy forms in different end-use markets and among various regions of the world. It is clear that in many regions of the world the supply of alternative forms of energy from domestic sources is not sufficient to meet demand, and that gap must be satisfied with imports. The international flow of crude oil has constituted the dominant share of international energy flows in the past, and this trend is expected to continue into the future. (See the second page of Figure 3-1.)

The availability and security of imported petroleum supplies is of major concern to oil-importing countries. The major factors influencing the flow of petroleum are briefly discussed below, and the world energy model constructed in subsequent chapters is used to simulate and forecast international energy flows based on these and other relevant factors in an equilibrium environment. That is, the model attempts to bring together supply and demand for energy for each region and to supplement the supply gap with imported energy. Thus, for the world as a whole, a network of energy flows can be determined.

Determinants of World Energy Flows. The major international oil companies operating in OPEC member countries have various sources of crude to meet the requirements of markets which they serve. Naturally, they are interested in using alternative crude sources so as to satisfy each market for petroleum product production using the least expensive, suitable sources of crude oil, subject to the restrictions of availability and other factors. These factors are relative crude production costs, posted prices, taxes, transport costs, quality of crude, refinery costs, product mix required by their markets, and other special factors, such as security of supply. But these are not the only factors, for the flow of oil is also affected by various nontechnical factors—some political and some stemming from ownership and corporate structure. In general, the main variables influencing the pattern of world oil flow are those described below.

First, the various world crude oils have different physical characteristics and yield patterns. Technology permits the yield of a crude oil to be adapted (within limits) to the market demand; however, this may involve significant costs. Second, the terms of most production concessions require oil companies to develop their concessions in the OPEC countries at a reasonable pace. This may take the form of fulfilling an agreed exploration program or, in the case of a producing oil field, it may take the form of increases in the volumes of liftings. Such restraints mean that oil companies are not entirely free to optimize their position by concentrating on the cheapest available source of crude oil. Third, some importing countries may encourage imports of crude oil from certain countries because of trade agreements or for balance-of-payments or security considerations. Fourth, the ownership of oil sources and marketing networks affects the flow of oil and its pricing. In broad terms, major international oil companies must give a higher priority to protecting their existing operations, admittedly in a growing world market, while newcomers to the industry can afford to concentrate more heavily on the cheapest source of crude and on the most profitable markets. Larger oil companies are willing to geographically diversify their sources of crude oil for security reasons, even at higher costs. Fifth, the actual physical movement of crude oil is not straightforward. A company's own crude oil is not necessarily the most convenient source of supply from the point of view of transportation, nor is it necessarily the most suitable type of crude for satisfying the requirements of the market it controls. Therefore, it is common to swap crude oil among companies in order to reduce cross-hauling and to increase flexibility of supply. Finally, the growing number of very large crude carrier (VLCC) tankers, deep-water ports, and transshipment terminals has changed the worldwide flow of petroleum.

Another important sector closely related to the international flow of energy is the international transportation network: the supply and demand for tanker capacity and transportation rates. In order to move crude oil, liquefied natural gas, and coal between countries or regions, adequate transportation facilities are required. The demand for transportation facilities can be easily determined once the international demand, supply, and flow of energy are determined. However, numerous factors determine the supply of transportation capacity. The world energy model incorporates these factors into its transportation network in order to determine the supply and demand for transportation capacity.

Determinants of Tanker Capacity Requirements. In the short run, tanker capacity cannot be readily increased, but the efficiency with which existing capacity is used can be improved by increasing operating speeds, increasing the efficiency at terminals, and reducing delays in loading and unloading. In the intermediate run, the inflow of dry cargo as well as of grain carriers into the market increases available tanker capacity. Significant changes in capacity occur in the long run as a result of changes in the number of orders for new ships and changes in the number of ships scrapped.

The supply of tanker tonnage (expressed in ton-miles per year) is basically dependent on cost, technical, and geographical factors.

Cost Factors

1. Tanker rates (spot and charter)
2. Size of tankers
3. Costs of crude oil storage
4. Turnaround time
5. Average capital invested in tankers

Technical Factors

1. Speed of tanker
2. Seasonal distribution of demand for tankers

3. Loading and unloading facilities
4. Average port time
5. Changes in other modes of distribution such as pipelines and transshipment terminals
6. Number of days per year off-hire
7. Scrappage

Geographical Factors

1. Origin and destination of tankers
2. Location of oil-producing and -importing countries
3. Type of coasts, rivers, and canals available
4. Changes in production and consumption patterns of crude oil, etc.

The number of orders placed for new ships in the long run depends on many factors. Some have an immediate impact; others have an impact with some time lag. Spot and charter freight rates, and expectations concerning those rates, influence the number of new ships ordered. Costs of shipbuilding, including interest rates, labor costs, alternative rates of return for money tied up in ships, and others, are of major significance in decisions to order new tankers. Further, the rate of technological obsolescence, the age distribution of existing vessels, scrappage rates, and vessel replacement are of major significance. Finally, the worldwide demand for oil, the pattern of tanker ownership among oil and tanker companies, and recently the entry of OPEC member countries into the tanker market will significantly influence long-run tanker capacity.

Price and Production Strategies of Oil-Exporting Countries

The first part of this chapter and the first two pages of Figure 3-1 described how equilibrium price, supply, and demand in the oil-importing countries can be determined and how much oil should be imported to balance the energy supply and demand in these countries. In other words, the net result of the first part of the analysis is to determine the demand for OPEC oil by oil-importing countries at different price levels. This demand is used as a guideline by OPEC member countries in formulating their price and production strategies. Such policy processes are graphically depicted in the second two pages of Figure 3-1 and described in more detail in the rest of this chapter.

The remainder of this chapter presents a framework for analyzing OPEC's future stability as well as the price, production, and investment strategies of its members as they are affected by the oil-importing countries, international oil companies, and individual OPEC countries themselves. OPEC strategies are affected by the domestic energy policies of oil-importing countries, the development of alternative energy resources, economic growth, balance of payments, the relative dependency of non-OPEC and OPEC member countries, the international flow and recycling of petrodollars, and the transfer of technology and know-how. These strategies are also affected by the relative abilities of the OPEC countries to absorb oil revenues for the purpose of consumption, investment, and imports; the size of their recoverable oil and gas reserves; their political motives; and the compatibility of their objectives.

External Factors Affecting OPEC Strategies

The external factors affecting OPEC price and production strategies are those associated principally with the international oil companies and oil-importing countries. The power of these participants is unequal and, of course, varies from one situation to another. Each participant attempts to maximize his benefits. As a result, conflicts of interest occur among the participants. These conflicts could be resolved through a bargaining process. But in whatever manner they are resolved, a balance must be achieved among many essential variables: political, economic, social, legal, and commercial.

The bargaining power of international oil companies and consuming countries vis-à-vis oil-producing countries is largely determined by variations in economic and political factors over a period of time, rather than merely by the power and tactics of negotiators at a particular moment.[8] The international oil companies have great economic power, and consequently a strong bargaining position. They influence the use of resources, product distribution, prices, the development of new technology, and the distribution of income. On the other hand, ample reserves of crude oil, economic development, growth of political and administrative expertise, and the unified goals and concerted actions of the OPEC countries all have progressively decreased the inequality in bargaining power between them and the consuming countries and oil companies.

In general, the demands of OPEC member countries have centered on higher returns through higher royalties, controlled production and exports, price increases, and participation in oil company activities. OPEC members prefer to receive their revenues in hard currencies and to refine their oil locally in order to increase revenues and provide additional employment.

The OPEC countries have made steady and remarkable gains in their negotiations with the international oil companies. Many oil concessions have been nationalized, and posted prices have been drastically increased. The interdependence of OPEC countries and international oil companies will continue at a high level as long as the former produces a significant portion of the world's oil and the latter transports, refines, and markets it. However, many signs indicate that the present institutional framework within which this interdependence is expressed will not continue indefinitely.

Internal Factors Affecting OPEC Strategies

In addition to external factors, individual OPEC members countries' price and production policies affect OPEC policies as a whole. Some OPEC countries compete with one another to a limited extent in order to increase their respective shares of crude oil exports. Others maintain firm production control policies which affect their market shares. For instance, the market share of crude oil exported by Middle Eastern OPEC countries with respect to total OPEC crude oil exports declined in the 1960s. This decline was basically due to the emergence and rapid growth of production in the African OPEC countries. In recent years, Libya, Iraq, and Kuwait have limited their production voluntarily, and this has helped other member countries to increase their shares.

The following factors are among the major determinants of bargaining power of each individual OPEC country.

1. The capacity to effectively absorb oil revenues into their respective domestic economies and the size of domestic development projects
2. The size of the population, economic infrastructure, skilled labor force, number of management experts, and the amount of nonpetroleum resources
3. The relative production cost and quality of crude, volume of crude oil and natural gas reserves, productive capacity, and the present production level of crude oil and natural gas
4. Production commitments to oil companies, historical patterns of production, equity ownership in the oil contracts, and proximity of crude sources to refining and marketing outlets
5. Political ideology, stability, military power, diplomatic and bureaucratic skills, degree of radicalism, and social values

6. Amount of investment in domestic and foreign projects, amount of foreign exchange holdings, the value of nonpetroleum exports, and the amount of investment income
7. New crude oil discoveries and development of alternative energy sources in non-OPEC countries, perception of future energy markets, and present value of future oil revenues
8. Relationships with oil-importing country governments, the oil industry, and other OPEC member country governments

Many adverse internal and external factors have impacted on OPEC during the past several years. Nevertheless, its ability to maintain unified price and production policies and to act as a price setter in the world oil markets has remained roughly intact. Non-OPEC suppliers are price takers, and their individual outputs have a negligible effect on world crude oil prices. However, because of economic and political differences among members, OPEC may not be as stable in the future as it has been recently. An optimum price and output strategy for one country may not necessarily be the same as for others. A country such as Venezuela with relatively small oil reserves and a large absorptive capacity for oil revenues is interested in a price-output policy which is different from that of Saudi Arabia, which has large oil reserves and a smaller capacity to absorb oil revenues.

Naturally, the potential of some OPEC members to become price setters is greater than others. However, there are not many OPEC members that can be considered price takers. The criteria for price leadership within OPEC is not only the size of crude oil reserves, but also factors such as the ability to absorb oil revenues and, most important of all, domestic and international political rivalry.

Once a price is set, other members will usually follow. However, it is possible for a price to be compromised by either price takers or price setters. Collusive price setting is more representative of the way that OPEC operates at present.

OPEC member countries are categorized in Figure 3-2 according to the relationship between their production potential and absorptive capacity. *Absorptive capacity* is defined by Adler[9] as "that amount of investment, or that rate of gross domestic investment expressed as a proportion of GNP, that can be made at an acceptable rate of return, with the supply of cooperant factors considered as given." The UN Economic Commission for Asia[10] defines absorptive capacity as setting a "limit to the amount of efficient investment physically possible ... particularly in the short run." Wells[11] defines absorptive capacity as the level of spending determined by a country's economic, social, and political constraints beyond which additional spending would cause adverse economic and/or social effects. Bridge[12] defines absorptive capacity as a short-term upper limit on the capacity of an economy to expand its real per-capita output. Adelman and Friis,[13] Chenery,[14] Morgan Guaranty,[15] OECD,[16] the U.S. Treasury,[17] and Yager and Steinberg[18] have more or less defined OPEC absorptive capacity for oil revenues in terms of the maximum volume of total imports that an oil-exporting country can effectively utilize in a given period of time. The concept of effective utilization is not well defined in these studies, and they estimate future import requirements (absorptive capacity) based on development plans of governments or simple extrapolation of recent import trends.

The countries in the third and fourth quadrants in Figure 3-2 are likely to be price takers, and those in the first and second quadrants are potential price setters. Countries in quadrant II have the highest likelihood of being price setters, and those in quadrant III have the highest likelihood of being price takers because of the relatively low absorptive capacity, production potential, and small influence on other members' policies. For instance,

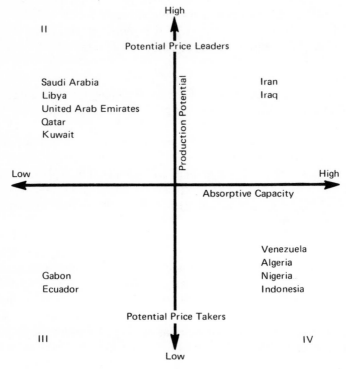

Figure 3-2. Absorptive Capacity, Production Potential, and Price Leadership of OPEC Member Countries.

Iran has a large population, vast economic development programs, and at the same time a relatively large reserve and production capacity for crude oil. Thus, it has been put in quadrant I. Libya and Saudi Arabia have large crude oil reserves and potential productive capacity, but they have small populations and their economic infrastructure is not strong enough to absorb a large amount of oil reserves. Thus, these countries have been categorized in quadrant II. Other countries have been classified in a similar way.

Given the wide differences in OPEC country interests, economic infrastructure, needs for oil revenues, productive capacities, and political motives, price and production decisions by individual members may cause OPEC countries to collectively produce crude oil in quantities more than or less than the amounts demanded from them by the oil-importing countries. Further, individual price and production decisions may be inconsistent with OPEC policy as a whole, and could weaken the organization and lead to higher world prices for crude oil. This means that if OPEC is to remain viable, it should adopt a formal or informal production-rationing policy and encourage each member to produce at or below the level allocated to it. If total OPEC production is higher than the demand for OPEC oil, the resulting "surplus" or "destruction" gap will exert a downward pressure on OPEC prices; if this situation continues for a long time it may eventually lead to destruction of the organization. An alternative possibility is that of individual members' price and production policy decisions resulting in a total OPEC production which is less than that demanded from it. The resulting "deficit" or "stability" gap will exert an upward pressure on world crude oil prices and lead to a more stable OPEC.

The final possibility is when total OPEC production is exactly equal to the oil demanded from it by the consuming countries. This requires the creation of a formal or informal production-prorationing scheme among OPEC member countries. Thus, the future stability of OPEC and its price and production policies can only be determined by the interaction of supply and demand for OPEC oil and the size of the gap created between them.

Given the substantial economic and political differences among OPEC member countries and their diverse economic infrastructures and different capabilities to absorb oil revenues into their economies, aggregate analysis of OPEC is not adequate for determining future price, production, and investment policies. Instead, analysis of each OPEC country's price, production, and investment policy as it relates to OPEC policies as a whole is essential. The above analysis emphasizes the superiority of individual country analysis as compared to treating OPEC as a whole. Further, the conventional revenue-maximization approach used for predicting OPEC's price and production policies is inadequate and does not reflect the behavior of OPEC decision makers.

A more plausible approach is for OPEC countries to set their price, production, and investment policies based on their relative capacity to absorb oil revenues into their domestic economies and to thus limit the amount of their foreign investment. It is reasonable to assume that oil revenues in excess of domestic development needs will be exposed to devaluation, inflation, expropriation, free loans or grants, excessive military expenditures, and downward pressure on world crude oil prices. Further, future generations will be denied adequate oil resources. Thus, it is desirable to examine this scenario and hypothesize that OPEC's price, production, and investment policies depend upon the policies of individual member countries which in turn depend upon their capacity to absorb oil revenues within their economies. Further, absorptive capacity varies among and within countries, among economic sectors, and over time. Thus, in order to measure the absorptive capacity of each country, econometric representation of major sectors of the economy including domestic investment, consumption, imports, exports, foreign investment, and military expenditures should be made.

The OPEC oil supply model presented later in this book can be used to forecast the future stability of OPEC and the production ration, absorptive capacity, and investment strategies of each OPEC member country simultaneously. Of course, one criterion for apportioning the demand for OPEC oil among its members is the relative capability to absorb oil revenues into their economies. The proposed analytical framework (OPEC oil supply model) can address the following questions:

1. How much crude oil will OPEC countries export individually and as a group at different price levels and under common or competitive objectives?
2. Would the production decisions of individual OPEC member countries lead to exports of crude oil greater in volume than the oil-importing countries demand from OPEC as a whole, given a price set by the cartel?
3. Would such individual production decisions (and likely oversupply) lead to a breakdown of the cartel and an eventual decrease in crude oil prices?
4. What production-prorationing scheme should be adopted by OPEC in order to discourage or avoid overproduction and breakdown of the cartel? In other words, is there any prorationing scheme that would maintain OPEC's stability?
5. Would there be any investable surplus available by the individual OPEC member countries and OPEC as a whole after their domestic

needs are satisfied, or would they borrow money in world financial markets?

More specific questions can also be addressed and evaluated within the proposed analytical framework:

6. How much capacity does each OPEC member have in absorbing revenues for imports, consumption, and investment?
7. What is the optimal crude oil prorationing scheme for OPEC and each member country?
8. How effective would be the side payment (e.g., a low-interest-rate loan) among OPEC countries in maintaining the cartel by not producing more than the assigned ration?
9. At what discount rate would OPEC members, in the aggregate or individually, be better off in keeping oil in the ground and financing their economic development through borrowing instead?
10. What are the likely future levels and composition of imports and exports of goods, services, and capital for each OPEC country?
11. What are the likely future levels of government and private investment and consumption for each OPEC country?
12. What would be the impact of changes in oil prices and world demand for oil on the sectoral economic growth of the individual OPEC countries?

In order to accomplish the above tasks, a modeling framework is constructed which encompasses various sectors of the economy including private and public consumption and investment, imports and exports by category, government taxes and petroleum revenues, crude oil production and exports, etc.

The outputs of the model are forecasts or simulations of each country's ability to absorb oil revenues for imports, consumption, investment, and each country's crude oil production or production ration. The model determines the amount of foreign investment (petrodollar surpluses) for each OPEC country based on its collective goal. Further, the model determines the "stability gap" or "destruction gap" between supply and demand for OPEC oil, which in turn is used as a measure of OPEC's future strength or weakness. The model can also be used to determine the amount of side payments (in the form of very low-interest rate loans) that one OPEC member could provide others in order to discourage them from producing beyond their ration. Establishment of a joint fund to accomplish this task has recently been considered by OPEC countries. Thus, it appears that a reasonable and effective production-rationing system with side payments may be adopted by OPEC to ensure its future stability.

The above discussion emphasizes that both low and high OPEC country capacities to absorb oil revenues have important implications for future OPEC price and production strategies as well as for the energy policies and programs to be adopted by oil-importing countries.

**Part II
World Energy Model: Oil-Importing
Countries**

4

Energy Demand and Supply Models

Part I presented a nonquantitative framework for analyzing the world energy economy for the benefit of general readers. Parts II and III present a quantitative description of the world energy model, which is based on that framework. Part II deals with energy supply, demand, and price determination in the oil-importing countries, and Part III deals with the price and production strategies of the oil-exporting countries (OPEC).

Energy models have been constructed in recent years by private, government, and academic institutions. Some deal with only a particular product, region, end-use, supply, or demand. Others deal with a single country rather than the international level, and still others deal with particular companies rather than industries. Most deal with only a part of the energy economy. That is, they consider the supply or demand of a particular product, end-use market, or region within a country without considering the integrated treatment of all these components in an integrated framework in a market clearing, or equilibrium, environment. The inadequacy of resources or the existence of localized energy problems has been the main reason for these piecemeal approaches to energy modeling and analysis. Fortunately, the Federal Energy Administration (FEA) has recognized the need for a comprehensive approach and has constructed an integrated framework for analysis of United States domestic energy problems.[1] Although the FEA domestic energy model has an extensive representation of the domestic energy economy, it lacks the international framework required to more adequately analyze the United States energy situation.[2] However, the author, while at FEA, did develop a partial international framework which is now used in conjunction with the domestic model and which is further developed in this book.

The necessity to analyze energy markets within an integrated framework has not gone unnoticed. The major international oil companies, including Exxon, British Petroleum, and Gulf, have modeled their international integrated operations through large-scale linear programming models. These models are used to analyze corporate planning problems, including optimum crude oil allocation among refineries, supply and demand balances, tanker requirements and chartering strategies, crude oil valuations, and investment requirements for production, refining, transportation, and marketing activities.[3] Most of these models are company-oriented and are designed to analyze company-related rather than industry issues. Further, they are mostly limited to oil operations and do not usually include other forms of energy. The British Petroleum model, for example, is a company-level oil model which has also been converted to an industry-level model by the Energy Research Unit of Queen Mary College[4] in order to analyze the international oil market. The converted form retains the level of refining and crude oil detail used by British Petroleum. The desirability of such detail for industrial analysis and the lack of nonpetroleum forms of energy in the model have been questioned by policy makers. Another modeling effort is by Houthakker and Kennedy.[5] This model is restricted to oil rather than to all energy forms. It has a simplified structure of the oil market at the world level. Its distinct advantage is the equilibrium framework used for analysis of this market. The Lorendas model developed by Rapoport is another effort at world energy modeling.[6] It has a fairly detailed representation of the supply and technology necessary for development of alternative energy resources. Its distinctive feature is that it is intertemporal. However, it does not adequately take into consideration the interaction of supply and demand. Other efforts have been devoted to analyzing certain segments of the international energy market and to dealing with particular problems, such as OPEC revenue-maximizing price strategies.

Most of the studies mentioned deal with the first two pages of Figure 3-1. That is, they attempt to model supply and demand for energy resources in the oil-importing countries and the need for crude oil imports from OPEC countries. But they do not treat these issues simultaneously with those that relate to OPEC's price, production, and investment strategies as they relate to OPEC's ability to absorb oil revenues for the purpose of importing, consuming, and investing.

The world energy model presented in this book deals with all the above issues. It is divided into two parts. The first deals with equilibrium supply, demand, and prices in the oil-importing countries and is discussed in this chapter and the next. The second part deals with price, production, and investment strategies of OPEC member countries and is discussed in Chapters 6 and 7.

That part of the world energy model which deals with oil-importing countries is an econometric, linear programming representation of various energy sectors of the oil-importing countries, including demand, refining, transportation, supply, flows, and pricing processes. The model is multiresource and multiregional in scope and considers the technological and economic interaction of primary energy resources (oil, gas, and coal) and demand for energy products. The model is a representation of energy supply and demand at the end of a planning period (say, 5 or 10 years). It does not trace the behavior of supply and demand for energy over time. It represents a competitive energy market in the consuming countries by means of upward-sloping supply and downward-sloping demand curves.

The equilibrium prices and quantities in each region are determined through market clearing processes. At equilibrium prices, suppliers satisfy exactly what consumers demand, no more and no less. This segment of the world energy model consists of several models: demand models, conversion technology models, logistic models, supply models, and an integrating model with a "market clearing algorithm" (see Figure 4-1). It should be noted that the demand curves (or demand side) are estimated by the demand model but the supply curves (or supply side) are estimated by the supply models as well as by the conversion and logistic models.

The demand models are used to estimate final demand for refined petroleum products, coal, natural gas, and electricity using constant price elasticities and forecasts of other relevant macroeconomic and demographic variables. The supply models consist of several other smaller models such as coal, oil, and gas. They are used to estimate supplies of these primary energy resources. The other models (conversion and

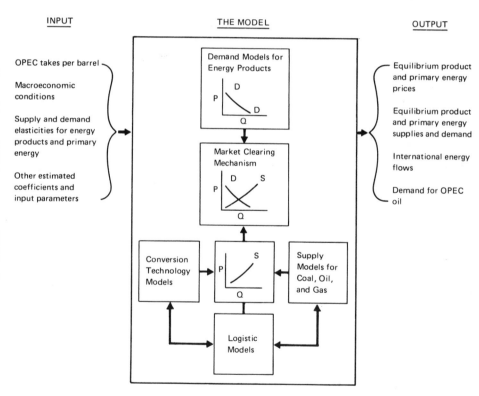

Figure 4-1. World Energy Model (Oil-Importing Countries)—Structure, Input, and Output.

logistic) may be considered a part of supply activities. They represent the transportation (flow) and transformation of primary energy products from their original forms to final products. Finally, the integrating framework and market clearing algorithm, or equilibrium process, bring together the supply and demand sides in order to estimate equilibrium prices and quantities.

The inputs to the first part of the world energy model (i.e., the part which deals with oil-importing countries) consist of supply and demand elasticities for alternative energy forms, forecasts of the relevant macroeconomic and demographic variables, and assumed alternative levels of OPEC crude oil prices per barrel. The outputs of the model include estimates of market clearing prices and quantities for primary energy and for final enegy products and electricity (approximately 15 energy products) for 20 geographical regions considered in the model. Further, the estimates of international energy flows and of the demand for OPEC oil by oil-importing countries at different levels of OPEC prices are generated by the model (see Figure 4-2). This chart indicates, from left to right, that the price-sensitive demands for various energy forms are forecasted as a function of major macroeconomic indicators. These demands are satisfied by price-sensitive supplies of alternative energy resources. Some of these resources will be transformed before the final demand for energy products is satisfied. The difference between domestic supply and demand for energy in each region (excess demand or supply) is imported or exported. These imports and exports generate the international flows of energy and the transportation network patterns.

Region and Resource Definitions

Geographic Regions

In order to reduce the size and complexity of the world energy model, the world is analyzed on a regional basis with all countries of the world grouped into 20 regions, as shown in Table 4-1. The model is flexible in regrouping these regions, as necessary. Since most of the data for the model are compiled at the country level, it is a relatively simple task to alter the assumed regionalization for any given study.

Several factors influence the selection of regions. First, the magnitude of United States supplies and demands and the access to this country via both the Atlantic and Pacific routes make it desirable to consider the United States as three regions. These regions are Petroleum Administration for Defense (PAD) districts 1 to 4, 5, and the Alaskan North Slope. Second,

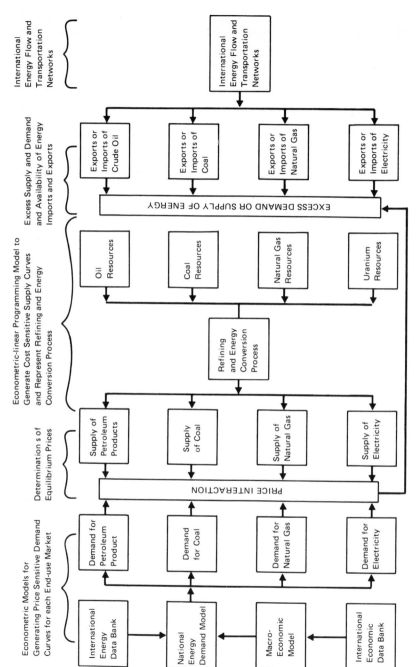

Figure 4-2. Major Components of World Energy Model—Oil-Importing Countries.

Table 4-1
World Regions

Regions	Countries
United States (PADs 1 to 4)	
United States (PAD 5)	
Alaska North Slope	
Canada	
Caribbean/Central America	Mexico, Guatemala, Honduras, Nicaragua, Costa Rica, El Salvador, Bahamas, Cuba, Dominican Republic, Haiti, Jamaica, Panama, Puerto Rico, Trinidad, Virgin Isles, others
Venezuela	
South America: Other	Argentina, Bolivia, Brazil, Chile, Columbia, Ecuador, Paraguay, Peru, Uruguay, others
Northern Europe	Belgium, Luxembourg, Denmark, France, West Germany, Ireland, Netherlands, United Kingdom, Austria, Finland, Iceland, Norway, Sweden, Switzerland
Southern Europe	Italy, Portugal, Greece, Spain, Turkey
North Africa	Algeria, Libya, Morocco, Tunisia, Egypt, Nigeria, Gabon, Camaroon, others
South Africa	Angola, Sudan, Chad, Congo, Ethiopia, Ghana, Kenya, Liberia, Rhodesia, Republic of South Africa, Southwest Africa, Mozambique, Tanzania, Zaire, Uganda, Zambia, Malagasy, others
Saudi Arabia	
Iran	
Middle East: Other	Bahrain, Iraq, Jordan, Kuwait, Lebanon, Oman, Neutral Zone, Qatar, Yemen, Syria, Abu Dhabi, Israel, others
Indonesia	
Japan	
Oceania	Australia, New Zealand, Guam, Wake Island, New Guinea, New Caladonia, American Samoa, others
Southwest Asia	Afghanistan, Bangladesh, Sri Lanka, India, Nepal, Pakistan, Brunei, Burma
Southeast Asia	Laos, Macau, Malaysia, Philippines, Singapore, Thailand, Taiwan, Hong Kong, Korean Republic, others
Soviet Bloc/China	China, North Korea, Mongolia, North Vietnam, Albania, Bulgaria, Czechoslovakia, East Germany, Hungary, Poland, Romania, Russia, Yugoslavia

major oil-exporting countries are given special consideration because of the relatively great impact of oil on the world's total energy situation. Regions which fall into this category include Venezuela, Saudi Arabia, Iran, other Middle Eastern countries and areas, North Africa, and Indonesia. Third, the magnitudes of energy demands in countries that belong to the Organization for Economic Cooperation and Development (OECD) warrant that they be analyzed separately or in groups. They include Canada, Northern Europe, Southern Europe, Oceania (primarily Australia and New Zealand), and Japan. Fourth, because of the relative isolation of the communist world with respect to energy and the paucity of data on their energy resources, the communist countries are considered as a single region entitled "Soviet Bloc/China." Fifth, the refining of crude oil in the Caribbean and its impact on product prices in the United States result in the categorization of Caribbean/Central America as a separate region. Finally, the remainder of the world, because of its relatively small supply and demand for energy resources, is divided geographically into four separate regions: South America (except Venezuela), South Africa, Southwest Asia, and Southeast Asia.

Resources and Products

That part of the world energy model which deals with oil-importing countries covers many energy products and primary forms of energy individually. The energy products and primary energy forms include crude oil (20 types), natural gas, hard coal, brown coal, electricity, liquefied petroleum gas, gasoline, jet fuel, distillate fuel oil, residual fuel oil, other refined products, tar sands, and oil shale. In addition, the demand for energy products is specified for each of four market sectors: residential-commercial, industrial, transportation, and electric generation.

The model computes the supplies and demands for these energy forms and market sectors from an extensive and highly disaggregated world energy data base maintained at the country level. This bank of detailed data includes approximately 125 different crude oils and up to 13 different refined products, depending upon the country for which the data are specified. The greatest disaggregation of product demand is maintained for the United States and the other OECD countries, and there are fewer categories of data for the communist and other non-OECD countries. The individual refined petroleum products available in the data bank are given in Table 4-2 by country groups.

The rest of this chapter describes the mathematical structure of the components of that part of the world energy model which deals with oil-importing countries.

Table 4-2
Refined Products

Aggregate	Non-OECD Countries	OECD Countries
Liquefied petroleum gas	Liquefied petroleum gas	Liquefied petroleum gas
Gasoline	Gasoline	Motor Gasoline
		Aviation gasoline
Jet fuel	Kerosene/jet fuel	Kerosene
		Kerosene/jet fuel
Distillate fuel oil	Distillate fuel oil	Distillate fuel oil
Residual fuel oil	Residual fuel oil	Residual fuel oil
Other	Lubricants/waxes	Lubricants
	Other	Paraffin waxes
		Bitumen
		Naphthas
		White spirit/SBP
		Other

Energy Demand Models

The world energy model (oil-importing countries) includes three energy demand models: the United States demand model, the non-OECD demand model, and the OECD (excluding the United States) demand model. The models are used to forecast energy demand for various geographic regions. The type of demand model used or constructed for any group of countries depends upon the level of energy demand and the availability of data for that group. OECD countries account for the major portion of free-world energy demand. A significant amount of relevant data is available for these countries.

United States Energy Demand Model

The United States energy demand model used is the one developed by the FEA for its Project Independence Evaluation System (PIES). An extensive description of this model appears in FEA's *1976 National Energy Outlook*.[7] A brief description of the model follows.

The United States energy demand model is used to forecast or simulate the demand for petroleum products, natural gas, coal, and electricity for each of nine census regions using econometric techniques. The prices of alternative energy forms and the levels of macroeconomic variables used in the model are treated as exogenous. The model generates demand elasticities for alternative energy products for each given set of prices for any year in the future. The major energy demand sectors considered in the model are residential-commercial, industrial, and transportation. This model is somewhat similar to the demand model for the OECD countries, which is presented later in this chapter. The demand for each fuel within each end-use market is assumed to be a function of the price of that fuel, the prices of substitute fuels, measures of the level of economic activity, and the time-lagged demand level.

The model for each of the three energy demand sectors has two parts: (1) an index of total energy demand, which depends on the absolute level of a deflated fuel price index and measures of the sectors' activity level (population and personal income), and (2) the ratio of each specific fuel demand to the total energy demand index as a function of the relative price of fuel. These general relationships are as follows:

$$\text{Ln } TQS = a_0 + a_1 \text{ Ln } TPS + a_2 \text{ Ln } YC + a_3 \text{ Ln } TQS_{-1}$$

$$\text{Ln } (FUQS/TQS) = a_0 + a_1 \text{Ln } (FUPS/TPS) + a_2 \text{ Ln } (FUQS/TQS)$$

where TQS = total energy demand quantity index in a demand sector
TPS = total energy price index
YC = per capita income
TQS_{-1} = lagged total energy quantity index for each demand sector
$FUQS$ = demand for particular energy form in a particular sector
$FUPS$ = price for a particular energy form in a particular demand sector

The last character (S) at the end of the above variables will be replaced by R, I, and T which stand for residential, industrial, and transportation demand sectors.

The elasticities generated by this model are not the same as the usual long-run elasticities presented in the literature. They are numerically calculated to reflect rolled-in price effects along a carefully specified future price trajectory which approximates price movements to an equilibrium consistent with given prices of imported crude oil for 1980 and 1985.

Non-OECD Demand Model

The demand model constructed for the non-OECD countries is simpler than the United States model. Growth in each country's demand for each product is projected independently of the demands for other products. Further, demand for any given product is an aggregate demand. That is, demand sectors (e.g., residential, commercial, transportation) are not treated separately. The model constructed for this purpose is the same for each country.

$$D_{it} = D_{i0}(1 + G_t)^{t \cdot IE_{it}} \left(\frac{P_{it}}{P_{i0}} \right)^{PE_{it}}$$

where D_{it} = demand for product i in year t
D_{i0} = demand for product i in the base year
G_t = growth rate of a country's economy in year t
t = planning years
IE_{it} = income elasticity of demand for product i in year t
PE_{it} = price elasticity of demand for product i in year t
P_{it} = price of product i in year t
P_{i0} = price of product i in the base year

This model does not incorporate the market share analyses used later in the OECD demand model, but its use is deemed appropriate for those countries whose demands for energy are relatively small.

OECD Demand Model

The OECD (excluding the United States) demand model used is that constructed by Adams and Griffin.[8] It is used to estimate or forecast demands for alternative energy forms (i.e., refined petroleum products, natural gas, coal, and electricity) based upon the degree of interfuel competition. Total demands for energy in each of three market sectors—transportation, residential-commercial, and industrial—are functions of gross domestic product, gross steel output, income, population, the price of energy relative to that for other products, and other variables. The market shares for individual fuels in each market are then determined based upon their relative prices and the degree of interfuel competition that exists in each country. (See Figure 4-3.)

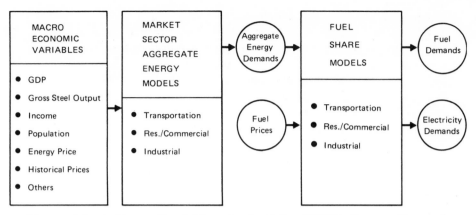

Figure 4-3. A Generalized Flowchart of the OECD Energy Demand Model.

The total energy demand model hypothesized for each country for each of the three sectors is:

$$E_{ij} = GDP^{\alpha 1i} \left(\frac{PE_{ij}}{P_j}\right) a_{2i}$$

where GDP = aggregate demand (real gross domestic product)
   E_{ij} = derived demand for energy (quantity)
   PE_{ij} = aggregate price of energy
   P_j = aggregate price level
   a_1 = constant income elasticity
   a_2 = constant price elasticity
   i = 1, 2, . . . , n sectors
   j = 1, 2, . . . , m countries

This formulation assumes constant price (a_2) and income (a_1) elasticities across all countries. However, the price and income elasticities of demand for energy vary substantially among different end-use markets because of the varying degrees of fuel substitution and capital or labor intensity of energy-consuming and -generating processes.

In order to determine the share of each fuel in total energy consumption in each end-use market, the following general model is used.

$$MS_{ki} = \frac{F_{ki}}{E_i} = F\left(\frac{P_1}{P_{\min}}, \frac{P_2}{P_{\min}}, \ldots, \frac{P_s}{P_{\min}}, Z\right)$$

where $k = 1, 2, \ldots, s$ fuels

$i = 1, 2, \ldots, n$ sectors

Z = a vector of nonprice variables affecting fuel shares

P_{min} = min $(P_1, P_2, \ldots, P_s)$ where all prices are in dollars per efficiency-adjusted Btu's

E = total energy demand

MS = market share of fuel

F = volume of fuel

P = price of fuel

There is a linear homogeneity in prices in the above relationship such that doubling of all prices has no effect on market shares. Further, the market shares for any country sum to 1.

The expected signs of coefficients for market share equations are not necessarily the same as those expected for usual (nonshare) demand equations. The own price elasticity in a usual demand equation for a particular fuel is expected to have a negative sign, and cross elasticities should have positive signs. This implies that total energy demand (E_i) is held constant. In market share equations, however, it is conceivable that a price reduction in a major fuel would result in a percentage increase in total energy demand (E_i) greater than the percentage increase for the specific fuel which was lowered in price.[9]

The general form of the demand and market share models differs significantly from the estimating equations presented below because of data limitations and other constraints.

The following sections briefly describe the modeling structure of each OECD (excluding the United States) end-use market.

Transportation Demand Sector. The aggregate level of energy consumed in the transportation sector (excluding gasoline and jet fuel) in OECD countries is derived as a function of gross domestic product (GDP), the aggregate price of energy in the economy, and the level of population in the country.

$$E = a_0 + a_1 GDP + a_2 POP + a_3 PE$$

where E = aggregate level of energy demand

GDP = real gross domestic product

POP = population

PE = aggregate price of energy

a_i = regression coefficients, $i = 0, 1, 2, 3$

The demands for gasoline and jet fuel are estimated separately. Demand for gasoline is determined by variables larger in number than for the rest of the transportation sector. The estimating equation is as follows:

$$GASC = GCAR \cdot CARC$$
$$= EXP (\log GCAR + \log CARC)$$
$$\log W = a_0 + a_1 \log GDPC + a_2 \log PPMG + a_3 \log PDEN$$
$$\log GCAR = a_0 + a_1 \log GDPC + a_2 \log PPMG + a_3 \log W$$
$$+ a_4 \log CARC$$
$$\log CARDC = a_0 + a_1 \log GDPC + a_2 (\log GDPC)^2 + a_3 \log CPRP$$

where $CARC$ = cars/capita
 W = average car weight
 $GDPC$ = GDP/capita
 $PPMG$ = price of premium motor gasoline
 $PDEN$ = population/country area
 $CPRP$ = car price/pound
 $GCAR$ = gasoline car
 $GASC$ = gasoline consumption per capita

Demand for jet fuel is assumed to grow at a constant rate.

Petroleum products encounter little competition from other energy forms in the transportation sector. Each product is used in a specialized type of engine and carrier.

Market share analyses of the transportation sector exclude gasoline and jet fuel. These fuels do not encounter appreciable interfuel competition. They are used primarily to transport individuals. The more general transportation category considered here includes transportation of both individuals and goods. Thus, the demand forecasts for gasoline and jet fuel are not estimated based on market share analyses. The types of fuels considered in market share analyses are:

1. Distillate fuel oil
2. Residual fuel oil
3. Coal
4. Electricity

The market shares of the individual fuels (except gasoline and jet fuel) in the sector are derived as a function of the prices of four of the alternative fuels and income per capita. The equation employed to estimate the market share (MS) for fuel (f) is

$$MS_f = b_0 + \sum_{i=1}^{4} b_i P_i + b_5 (GDP/POP)$$

where P_i ($i = 1, 2, 3, 4$) are the prices of four fuels (coal, distillate, residual, and electricity) and b_i ($i = 1, 2, 3, 4$) and b_5 are regression coefficients.

Residential-Commercial Demand Sector. OECD's (excluding the United States) demand for energy in the residential-commercial sector is the sum of the demands for space heating, water heating, air conditioning, cooking, refrigeration, lighting, etc. Interfuel competition is quite intense in this market. Distillate fuel oil, gas, and electricity compete in space heating; gas and electricity compete in cooking and air conditioning; and electricity is the principal energy source for lighting.

The fuels consumed in the residental-commercial sector are

1. Coal
2. Natural gas
3. Kerosene
4. Distillate fuel oil
5. Electricity

Aggregate energy demand (E) excluding electricity is assumed to be a function of income per capita (GDP/POP), the aggregate price of energy (PE), and that portion of the GDP which is due to agriculture (AGG). The equation is as follows:

$$E = a_0 + a_1 \log (GDP/POP) + a_2 \log PE + a_3 AGG$$

where $i = 0, 1, 2, 3$ are the regression coefficients.

Electricity demand is estimated independently of the other forms of energy. The estimating equation for per capita residential electricity demand (REL/POP) is

$$\log (REL/POP) = b_0 + b_1 \log (GDP/POP) + b_2 \log (PELAR/P)$$

where the real price of electricity ($PELAR/P$) is measured by the average residential price ($PELAR$) deflated by the GDP deflator (P).

The market shares of the alternative fuels (excluding electricity are then given by

$$MS_f = b_0 + \sum_{i=1}^{4} b_i \log P_i + b_5 \log (GDP/POP) + b_6 AGG$$

where P_i ($i = 1, 2, 3, 4$) are the prices of coal, natural gas, kerosene, and distillate fuel oil.

Industrial Demand Sector. Industrial sector energy use represents a large portion of the fuel consumed in most of the OECD economies. This sector includes all manufacturing industries with the exception of electricity generation. The determination of energy demands for this sector is divided into two parts: iron and steel industries and other industries. Available OECD data permit segregating iron and steel production fuel demand from the demand by the other industries. This procedure enables the model to better predict the consumption of energy resources within the critical iron and steel industry, which is more energy-intensive than most of the other industries.

Fuel consumption in the iron and steel industry is computed as a function of the prices of the competing fuels, the price of energy relative to the prices of other products, and the gross steel output of each country's economy. The fuels whose demands are estimated for this industry are coal, natural gas, residual fuel oil, and electricity.

Aggregate energy consumption in the iron and steel industry is estimated as a function of gross steel output (GSO) and the price of energy (PE).

$$E = a_0 + a_1\, GSO + a_2\, PE$$

The market shares of the four fuels in that industry are estimated as a function of each of their prices and the GSO for the country being considered. The equation used is

$$MS_f = b_0 + \sum_{i=1}^{4} b_1\, (P_i) + b_5 \log GSO$$

where P_i ($i = 1, 2, 3, 4$) are the prices of the four fuels—coal, natural gas, residual fuel oil and electricity.

Energy consumption within the other industries is not related to the production of any particular commodity, such as steel. It is taken to be a function of a country's gross domestic product, an energy intensity index of the overall set of commodities (excluding steel) produced within the country, and the price of the energy relative to the price of other products. The equation used to estimate aggregate energy demand for these industries is

$$E = a_0 + a_1 \log GDP + a_2 \log PE + a_3\, EINT$$

where $EINT$ is the energy intensity index described above.

The market shares of the individual fuels are estimated as a function of the prices of the four fuels used in the iron and steel industry and the gross domestic product. The equation used is

$$MS_f = b_0 + \sum_{i=1}^{4} b_i\, (P_i) + b_5 \log GDP$$

Refining and Other Energy Conversion Models

This section describes the transformation of primary energy resources (oil, gas, and coal) into the final products modeled in the world energy model. These transformations include the refining of crude oils into such products as gasoline, distillate and residual fuel oil, LPG and other products, and the transformation of coal, natural gas, and residual fuel oil into electricity.

The main objective of the refining model is to determine the world flow and movement of crude oil by selecting among crudes with different quality, specifications, and availability so as to satisfy the given demand for petroleum products at a minimum cost. The model also determines new refinery expansion capacity and investment requirements. However, in the real world there are certain restrictions on the availability of all types of crude to particular refining/marketing regions. These constraints are physical, political, economic, contractual, and corporate.

Physical constraints, including productive capacity (i.e., inadequate development wells, pipelines, loading terminals, etc.), create short-run bottlenecks for crude availability. Because of political repercussions oil companies cannot make substantial changes in their geographical crude production patterns. Bilateral trading and investment agreements between producing and consuming countries influence the availability of all types of crude to a refining/marketing region. Corporate crude positions as well as degree of self-sufficiency of individual crude oil-producing companies differ in each of the major producing regions. Corporate crude availabilities can be affected by internal lifting agreements in the major concession areas of the oil-producing countries or by long-term purchase contracts. A company short on crude can rapidly develop a field in which it has majority interest, while a company long on crude may have greater difficulty if it is to maintain its offtake share in a multicompany concession. Further, crude requirements outside each refining region influence the availability of crude to the region under study.

Finally, and most important, is the profit that a crude can generate in a particular refining/marketing region. The higher the profit for a crude, the greater the preference to produce that crude in the region. The profitability of a crude is a function of many variables including exploration, development, production cost, government taxation, transportation differentials, crude quality, price differentials in petroleum products, etc. With regard to crude quality, the model indicates that the relative crude value is a function of crude slates. As the share of an individual crude increases, its value tends to drop relative to other crudes, since it is no longer possible to take advantage of its desirable qualities. For example,

Libyan crude is worth very little more in a market that has a relatively large demand for fuel oil than any other crude, since its more valuable middle-distillate content must be partly downgraded to fuel oil.

The following subsection describes the structure and components of the refinery models.

Refining Models

The refining industry can be modeled in one of two ways. One method requires building models of all refineries in the region under study. Each model represents major process units in a refinery. Although this type of model preserves the identity and individual characteristics of each refinery, it is easily seen that the model's size and complexity grow substantially with each additional refinery.

The alternative modeling technique involves creating a single refinery model that represents the "average" refinery in the region being studied. Sizes and process parameters for each unit in the average refinery are determined by averaging unit data for all refineries in the region.

Refineries that process similar crudes and produce similar products have basically the same configuration. Geographic location, crude availability, and product demand pattern are the major determinants of refinery configuration. The aggregate-average model is an appropriate tool for studying refineries in regions where refinery configuration and crude availability are reasonably similar. The pattern of expansion predicted by such a model will reflect the behavior expected by most refiners in that region, even though the characteristics of individual refineries are partially obscured in the aggregating process. This is the type of refinery model used in the world energy model.

The relative amounts of gasoline, fuel oils, and lubricating oils yielded by various crude oils vary considerably. Thus, the volumes and properties of refinery streams will differ according to the crude being processed. This has a significant impact on individual unit operations. Consequently, a refinery's configuration and operation are quite dependent on the relative mix of crudes that it charges.

The world energy model divides the world into 20 regions. Ten are considered as major refining centers. The refining activities of these ten regions are represented in the world energy model through 12 composite refinery linear programming models. That is, each refinery center is represented by a single refinery that represents the aggregate of the present refineries in the region and which has the capability of expanding its capacity when necessary. The regions for which separate refinery models have been constructed are as follows:

United States (PADs 1 to 4)	Southern Europe
United States (PAD 5)	Japan
Caribbean	South East Asia
Canada	Middle East
Northern Europe	Oceania

The refinery operations in those remaining free-world regions (the other eight regions) for which there are only small refining operations are not modeled explicitly. They are treated as having fixed capabilities for transforming each available crude oil into a specified slate of refined products.

The refining models link the demand for finished products generated with the energy demand models to the logistic and supply models. The components of the refinery models are described below.

Refinery Process Unit Capacities. Each composite refinery model represents the aggregate refineries in a refining/marketing region and contains all types of refinery processes used in that region. Although not all refineries in a region use the same processes, their overall refining operations are sufficiently similar so that they can be represented in an aggregate refinery. A large number of refinery processes are used in refineries, but for the sake of simplicity and manageability only the most important are presented in the refinery flowchart (Figure 4-4). Additional ones are included in the model, and even more can be added as desired.

The following types of processes are those most widely used in refineries. A flow diagram of a typical refinery is presented in Figure 4-4.

Atmospheric distillation	Alkylation
Vacuum distillation	Polymerization
Visbreaking	Isomerization
Catalytic cracking	Coking
Thermal cracking	Hydro-desulfurization
Hydro cracking	Hydrogen plant
Catalytic reforming	Hydrotreater of distillate
Thermal reforming	

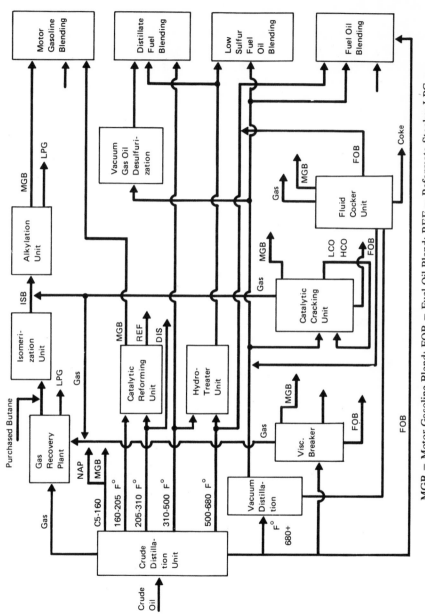

Figure 4-4. Refinery Flowchart.

MGB = Motor Gasoline Blend; FOB = Fuel Oil Blend; REF = Reformate Stocks; LPG = Liquefied Petroleum Gas; NAP = Naphtha; DIS = Distillate Fuel Blend

Some refining processes are not included in the model, such as lube oil plants. These processes are used for making specialized products in certain refineries.

Process Unit Operating Costs. In the refinery linear programming models, only variable costs play a role in selecting among crudes. Fixed costs have no bearing on the final outcome. The only time that fixed costs are taken into consideration is when new refineries are built or present refining capacities are expanded.

The variable operating cost per barrel of feed for each possible process is an input to the model. This cost includes costs of catalysts, chemicals, tetraethyl lead, corrosion due to sulfur in crude oils, fuels, cooling towers, power, maintenance, labor, acid, etc.

Petroleum Product Specifications. Finished petroleum products are classified according to a large number of characteristics. Typical specifications for major petroleum products are presented in Table 4-3.

The major specifications for motor gasoline are octane rating and vapor pressure. Further, gasoline must be sweet, must be low in sulfur, should not have a final boiling point exceeding about 400°F, and should contain less than 3 cc/gal of tetraethyl lead (TEL).

The specifications for naphthas vary according to their intended use, for example, to make aromatics, ethylene, ammonia, etc. Naphthene and aromatic-rich naphthas are superior for aromatic manufacture, but

Table 4-3
Typical Petroleum Product Specifications

Motor Gasoline:	Octane number	88 to 100 research octane
	Final boiling point	400°F maximum
	50% evaporated	240°F maximum
	Vapor pressure	10 lb maximum
	Lead content	3 cc/gal maximum
Gas Oil:	Final boiling point	725°F maximum
	Distillation	90% recovered minimum at 675°F
	Flash point	150°F minimum
	Pour point	20°F maximum
	Cetane number	50 minimum
	Sulfur	0.5 to 1.0% maximum
Residual Oil:	Sulfur	Variable—unlimited to under 1%
	Flash point	150°F minimum
	Pour point	Variable—often 75°F maximum
	Viscosity range	Variable—300 to 5000 Redwood
	Heating value	18,000 Btu/lb minimum

paraffinic or hydrogen-rich naphthas are preferred for ammonia, methanol, etc.

Kerosene should have a smoke point exceeding 23, a specific gravity below 0.82, and sulfur below 0.13 percent.

Sulfur content and pour point are the two most restrictive specifications for gas oils. These specifications vary with government policies and climatic conditions; e.g., a lower pour point is preferred for colder climates. Because of pollution control regulations, residual fuel oil should not exceed a certain maximum sulfur content.

Crude Oil Qualities and Yields. Crude oil is not a homogeneous commodity. Hundreds of different types can be recognized throughout the world. Each generates a somewhat different product yield, and some require different and specialized equipment in order to be processed. Refiners attempt to find the most economical way of converting a given type of crude oil into a given set of products. The characteristics of some crudes are presented in Table 4-4. The differences in characteristics are quite apparent. Bachequero crude oil from Venezuela is a very heavy crude that yields about 79 percent residual fuel oil (680°F+), while Hassi-Messaoud crude oil from Algeria is a light crude and yields only 24 percent residual (680°F+). Of course, since the latter crude oil yields a high percentage of more expensive light products (e.g., gasoline), it is a more valuable crude than the former.

Further, among crude oils which have a relatively high yield of residual fuel, the ones with less sulfur content are at a premium in markets which have environmental restrictions. Minas crude oil from Indonesia and Arabian heavy both have relatively high yields of residual fuel oil (58.5 and 55.8 percent respectively). However, Minas crude is at a premium in Japanese markets relative to Arabian heavy crude because the former has 0.12 percent and the latter has about 4.3 percent sulfur in their residual fraction (680°F+). Many additional comparisons could be made, and it is a common practice among refiners to do so.

Each type of crude is not suitable to produce all types of petroleum products. For instance, some crude oils cannot be used to produce lube oil or asphalt. Again, if a refiner attempts to produce required volumes of fuel oil from 45° API crude, it can be done, but only by either sacrificing valuable distillate for fuel oil or incurring extensive costs of downstream processing if the refiner attempts to obtain enough low-boiling material from 10° API crude oil. Further, some processes are interrelated. Thus, polymerization or alkylation can be performed in refineries which have cracking plants. Finally, not all refineries are equipped to handle high-sulfur crude oils.

All crude oils which enter into a refining/marketing region are processed

Table 4-4
Characteristics of Selected Crude Oils

Characteristics of Various Crude Oils and Their Fractions	Types of Crude Oil				
	Agha Jari–Iranian Light	Arabian Heavy	Arabian Light	Bachequero–Venezuela	Danish North Sea
Gravity, API	33.8	28.5	34.0	13.5	30.4
Sulfur, Wt %	1.4	2.8	1.8	2.4	0.2
Pour Point, °F	-20	-30	-30	-10	-15
Distillation, Wt % (% Yield)					
57°F-205°F	7.6	6.75	8.2	0.74	5.8
205°F-310°F	9.0	6.9	8.6	0.51	8.5
310°F-500°F	18.4	13.9	17.6	6.3	18.7
500°F-680°F	17.9	15.2	17.9	13.2	19.1
680°F+	46.1	55.8	46.7	79.2	47.4
Gravity in 680°F+ (API)	17.0	11.1	16.2	5.8	20.0
Sulfur in 680°F+ (wt %)	2.4	4.3	2.9	3.3	0.5
Pour Point in 680°F+	75	65	70	105	75
Nickel in 680°F+ (PPM)	79	41	8.7	80	14
Vanadium in 680°F+ (PPM)	198	125	33	579	2.4

Types of Crude Oil

Characteristics of Various Crude Oils and Their Fractions	Gash Saran–Iranian Heavy	Hassi-Messaoud–Algeria	Khafji–Neutral Zone	Minas–Indonesia	Tiajuana–Venezuela	Zarzaitin–Algeria
Gravity, API	31.0	45.5	27.9	35.3	24.7	42.5
Sulfur, Wt %	1.6	0.14	2.88	0.9	1.8	0.08
Pour Point, °F	−5	−12	−31	90	−28	16
Distillation, Wt % (% Yield)						
57°F-205°F	7.1	15.4	6.9	3.0	4.5	9.9
205°F-310°F	7.7	14.0	6.7	5.6	6.1	12.0
310°F-500°F	16.9	23.2	13.9	14.7	12.5	23.0
500°F-680°F	15.7	19.4	15.0	17.8	16.6	19.3
680°F+	50.9	24.2	55.9	58.5	59.5	33.6
Gravity in 680°F+ (API)	14.0	22.2	11.1	27.0	13.4	24.9
Sulfur in 680°F+ (wt %)	2.6	0.4	4.5	0.12	2.5	0.1
Pour Point in 680°F+	75	74	65	120	45	66
Nickel in 680°F+ (PPM)	84	0.2	35	18	45	2.2
Vanadium in 680°F+ (PPM)	207	0.5	100	0.5	400	3.1

in their own best way for the production of various products, and only the average yields from all the crude oils should match the market demand.

The profit made by each refiner from his crude oil should be nearly the same as the profits made by every other refiner from their respective crude oils. This must be true, or, else certain crude oils would be rejected from the region. A low-gravity API crude oil is usually worth less than a high-gravity API crude oil, but the delivered price of low-gravity oil (less discount) must be low enough to permit it to compete with higher-gravity oils which are more valuable. Changes in product prices have little effect on the market share of each crude in a region, unless the prices of some products change greatly with respect to prices of other products. The recent increased demand for low-sulfur fuel oil illustrates how a change in the specifications of one product can alter the relationship between values of crude oils.

The yield pattern of a particular crude oil not only is a function of its properties but also depends upon the yields of all crudes serving that particular refining/marketing region.

Crude Types and Availabilities. A large number of crude oils with different characteristics are used by refineries in each refining/marketing region. To manage a model which incorporates all these crudes would be a formidable task, and the data collection problems would be extensive. For these reasons, certain crudes are used to represent others in both quantity and quality in the refineries. The characteristics as well as the maximum availabilities of these crudes are used as inputs to the refinery model. Crude availabilities are generated by the supply model. A sample of some types of aggregate crude oils in the model is listed in Table 4-5 together with the individual types that make up the aggregates.

New Capacity and Investment. The refinery model incorporates the existing capacities of all refinery processes and provides for additions to these capacities when the product demand to be accommodated is greater than can be provided by existing capacities. Variables are included to allow for additions to each unit and process together with their associated investment costs.

Although the modeling structure for new capacity and investment consists only of balance rows and representation of investment cost coefficients in the objective function, supporting data are substantial for building incremental (or marginal) cost curves for new capacity. A capital recovery factor is used in each refinery model for calculating the costs associated with building incremental units of capacity. This reflects the percentage of initial investment which must be recovered each year in order to realize a predetermined return on original investments. Finally, an implicit, or opportunity, cost for new capacity investment is determined by applying the capital recovery factor to total production costs.

Table 4-5
Selected Crude Oils in the World Energy Model

Aggregate	Components
Alaska North Slope	Alaska Crude
U.S. West Coast Mix	San Joaquin Valley, Kern River, Los Angeles Basin (Willmington), California Coastal Avg. (Ventura)
U.S. Low-Sulfur Mix	Oklahoma Sweet, Wyoming Light (Grass Creek), Kansas "A," West Texas Light (Scurry County), Gulf Coast, East Texas, South Louisiana
U.S. High-Sulfur Mix	Wyoming Heavy (Steamboat Butte), Oklahoma "S" crude, West Texas Heavy, West Texas Sour
Canadian Mix	Pembina, Swan Hill, Inter-Prov. Mix
Venezuela Light	Lagomar, Tia Juana Light
Venezuela Heavy	Bachequero, Monagas, Tia Juana Medium
North Sea	Ekofisk
Indonesian Mix	Minas, Duri, Lirik
Russian Export	Black Sea Special, Baltic Special
Libyan	Amal, Nafoora, Sarir
Algerian	Hassi Messaoud, Zarzaitine, Ohanet
Nigerian	Forcados, Bonny
Iranian Light	Agha Jari, Darius
Iranian Heavy	Gach Saran
Iraqi Mix	Kirkuk, Basrah
Kuwait Export	Kuwait Crude
Arabian Light	Arabian Light, Berri
Arabian Heavy	Safaniya, Khursaniyah
Abu Dhabi Mix	Murban, Umm Shaif, Zakum

Typical Refinery Model

The structure of refinery linear programming models used in the world energy model is very detailed and cannot be presented in this book in its entirety. However, since there is a great similarity in modeling the refineries in various regions, an example of a typical refinery model is presented in order to acquaint the reader with the general outline of the modeling structure.

A linear programming refinery model consists of a set of linear relationships which defines the restrictions on a system of refinery variables. The variables in a refinery model include the rates of inflow of feedstocks to various refinery process units and the respective outflows (finished or intermediate products) and operating conditions of the units.

In order to demonstrate some of the relationships in the refinery linear programming model, a very simple example is given below. A hypothetical composite refinery is generated by aggregating the existing refineries in a particular region. Figure 4-5 presents the structure of such a refinery. The following operating data and information are available for this hypothetical refinery.

Crude Availabilities. Two types of crudes, A and B, are available to the refinery at prices of $11.60 and $11.00 per barrel, respectively. Because of the high sulfur and metal content of crude type B, it can account for only 20 percent of the total crude oil input to the refinery. The maximum availability of crude type A is 130,000 barrels per day (130 Mbbl/D).

Crude Distillation. The crude distillation unit capacity is 125 Mbbl/D, and it can process both types of crudes for maximum distillate production by changing the operating conditions of the unit. Each barrel of crude costs $0.50 to be processed. Table 4-6 shows the yield pattern of crude oils under the operating modes. This table shows that if one barrel of crude type B is processed under the maximum distillate mode, its yield will be 25, 35, and 35 percent of straight-run naphtha, distillate, and residual fuel oil, respectively. The remaining 5 percent accounts for refinery fuel and refinery gains or losses.

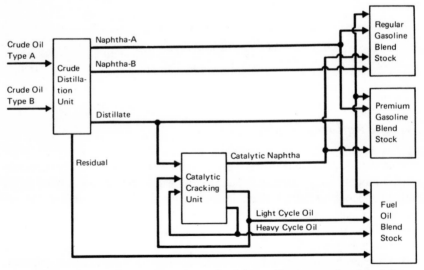

Figure 4-5. Refinery Flowchart for Linear Programming Model.

Table 4-6
Typical Yield Pattern for Types A and B Crude Oils

	Crude A		Crude B	
	Distillate	Fuel Oil	Distillate	Fuel Oil
Straight-run naphtha	0.40	0.15	0.25	0.25
Straight-run distillate	0.35	0.25	0.35	0.25
Atmospheric bottom residue	0.20	0.55	0.35	0.45
Fuels and losses (net)	0.05	0.05	0.05	0.05

Catalytic Cracking. The catalytic cracking unit has a more sophisticated operation than the atmospheric distillation unit, since it has a feedback (or recycling) operation. The feedstocks to catalytic cracker are straight-run distillate and light- and heavy-cycle oils which have been returned for recycling. The operating characteristics of the catalytic cracker are presented in Table 4-7. The first three rows of the table represent the yield of the catalytic cracker unit. The fourth represents the proportion of feedstock recycled, and the last represents the variable operating cost for processing a barrel of input in the catalytic cracker. The first column of Table 4-7 shows that an input of one barrel of straight-run distillate to the catalytic cracker yields 0.8 bbl (barrel) of naphtha, 0.4 bbl of light-cycle oil, and 0.5 bbl of heavy-cycle oil. There is a refinery gain resulting from the expansion of the input stock. Further, 0.5 bbl of the input stock is recycled within the catalytic cracker. It costs $0.20 to process 1 bbl of an input stock in the catalytic cracker.

Blending Final Products. The output generated by various process units (in this example, distillation and catalytic cracking) is blended together to make final products in quantities and at specifications required by the market. The specifications of intermediate feedstocks are given in Table 4-8, and the specifications and quantity requirements for final products are given in Table 4-9. For instance, the market requires that premium gasoline have at least 92 octane. Refiners should, therefore, blend the input stocks (with varying octane) in such a proportion as to meet final octane requirements. Reid vapor pressure (RVP) is another important specification of gasoline, in addition to the octane number. The viscosity specification is important for fuel oils.

Given the above operating data for the composite refinery, a series of constraints in terms of linear equalities and inequalities can be formulated in such a way as to meet the quantity and quality specification requirements for final products, given the limited availability of crude and processing

Table 4-7
Catalytic Cracking Operating Characteristics

	Straight-Run Distillate	Light-Cycle Oil	Heavy-Cycle Oil
Catalytic naphtha, bbl	0.8	0.7	0.2
Light-cycle oil, bbl	0.4	—	0.6
Heavy-cycle oil, bbl	0.5	0.5	—
Internal recycle	0.5	0.2	0.1
Variable operating cost, $/bbl	0.20	0.25	0.30

Table 4-8
Intermediate Feedstocks: Quality Specifications

	Motor Octane	RVP	Viscosity Blending Number
Straight-run naphtha A	86	13	—
Straight-run naphtha B	83	10	+5
Catalytic naphtha	94	6	—
Distillate	—	—	+2
Light-cycle oil	—	—	+1
Heavy-cycle oil	—	—	−1
Residual	—	—	−5

Table 4-9
Final Products: Quantity and Quality Specifications

	Demand, Mbbl/D	Price, $/bbl	Octane Rating	RVP	Viscosity Blending Number
Regular gasoline	At least 15	14.0	At least 89	12 maximum	—
Premium gasoline	At most 40	15.0	At least 92	10 maximum	—
Fuel oil	At most 60	9.0	—	—	0.0 minimum

capacities and the other requirements and constraints mentioned. These relationships are most conveniently presented in matrix form (Table 4-10). The column names are the variables in the refinery model, which are described in Table 4-11. The row names are the names of the constraints. They are defined in Table 4-12. The elements of the matrix represent the coefficients of the relevant variables. The right-hand side (RHS) column vector represents the bounds on the constraints with less than, greater than, or equal signs. The following paragraphs briefly describe how the above relationships are formulated and how the coefficients are calculated.

1. Material Balance Constraints. The first eight equations in the linear programming matrix are material balance equations of the process and stocks within the refinery. The plus signs of the coefficients represent outputs, and minus signs represent inputs. For instance, equations (1) and (2) are the material balances for straight-run naphtha from crude type A and type B respectively. The third equation is for straight-run distillate. As an example, the third equation can be written and interpreted as follows:

$$(1)(FDIS) + (1)(CATD) - (0.35)(CRAD) - (0.25)(CRAF)$$
$$- (0.35)(CRBD) - (0.25)(CRBF) = 0$$

The sources of distillate are from two types of crudes (types A and B) processed in two operating modes (fuel and distillate) with their respective yield coefficients, and the destinations of the distillate are to fuel oil blend and catalytic cracker for further processing.

2. Process Unit Balances. Equation (9) in the matrix shows that type A crude oil should be at least 4 times greater in volume than crude B (or crude B should constitute no more than 20 percent of total crude input). Equations (10) and (11) are capacity constraints for distillate and catalytic cracking units. Equation (10) indicates that the amount of crude charges to distillation units cannot be greater than 125 Mbbl/D. Catalytic cracking equation (11) states that for every 1-bbl input of distillate, 0.8 bbl is recycled internally. Therefore, the input quantity (CATD) should be multiplied by 1.8 in order to arrive at the total flow through the catalytic cracking unit.

3. Product Blending Constraints. Final petroleum products, in terms of both quantity and quality, are made by blending intermediate stocks. Octane number and RVP are important characteristics for gasoline, and viscosity linear blending number is important for fuel oil. Equations (12), (15), and (18) are final-product production requirement constraints, i.e., at least 15 Mbbl/D of regular gasoline and at most 40 Mbbl/D and 60 Mbbl/D of premium gasoline and fuel oil should be produced. Equations (13), (14),

Table 4-10
Linear Programming Matrix of a Hypothetical Refinery Model

| | Row Name | Equation No. | RHS | Premium Gasoline Blend | | |
				PNAA	PNAB	PNAC
Material Balance Constraints	NAPA	1	0 =	1		
	NAPB	2	0 =		1	
	DIST	3	0 =			
	RISD	4	0 =			
	NAPC	5	0 =			1
	CATL	6	0 =			
	CATH	7	0 =			
	CRDA	8	130 ⩾			
Crude Distillation Constraints	CBAL	9	0 ⩾			
	CCAP	10	125 ⩾			
Catalytic-Cracking Constraints	CATF	11				
Regular Gasoline Constraints	RQUN	12	15 ⩽			
	ROCT	13	0 ⩾			
	RRVP	14	0 ⩾			
Premium Gasoline Constraints	PQUN	18	40 ⩾	1	1	1
	POCT	16	0 ⩾	6	9	−2
	PRVP	17	0 ⩾	3	0	−4
Fuel Oil Constraints	FQUN	15	60 ⩾			
	FVIS	19	0 ⩽			
Profits	Σ	20		−15.0	−15.0	−15.0

	Regular Gasoline Blend			Fuel Oil Blend				
RNAA	RNAB	RNAC	FNAB	FDIS	FRES	FLCY	FHCY
1							
	1		1				
				1			
					1		
		1					
						1	
							1
1	1	1					
3	6	−5					
1	−2	−6					
			1	1	1	1	1
			5	2	5	1	−1
−14.0	−14.0	−14.0	−9.0	−9.0	−9.0	−9.0	−9.0

Table 4-10 (cont.)

	Row Name	Equation No.	RHS	Crude Distillation Unit				Catalytic Cracking		
				CRAD	CRAF	CRBD	CRBF	CATD	CATL	CATH
Material Balance Constraints	NAPA	1	0 =	−.20	−.15					
	NAPB	2	0 =			−.25	−.25			
	DIST	3	0 =	−.35	−.25	−.35	−.25	1		
	RISD	4	0 =	−.40	−.55	−.35	−.45			
	NAPC	5	0 =					−.8	−.7	−.2
	CATL	6	0 =					−.4	1	−.2
	CATH	7	0 =					−.5	−.5	1
	CRDA	8	130 ≥	1	1					
Crude Distillation Constraints	CBAL	9	0 ≥	−.25	−.25	1	1			
	CCAP	10	125 ≥	1	1	1	1			
Catalytic-Cracking Constraints	CATF	11						1.8	1.7	1.2
Regular Gasoline Constraints	RQUN	12	15 ≤							
	ROCT	13	0 ≥							
	RRVP	14	0 ≥							
Premium Gasoline Constraints	PQUN	18	40 ≥							
	POCT	16	0 ≥							
	PRVP	17	0 ≥							
Fuel Oil Constraints	FQUN	15	60 ≥							
	FVIS	19	0 ≤							
Profits	Σ	20		12.10	12.10	11.5	11.5	.20	.25	.30

Table 4-11
List of Variable Names in the Refinery Linear Programming Model

PNAA	=	Naphtha from type A crude to premium gasoline
PNAB	=	Naphtha from type B to premium gasoline
PNAC	=	Catalytic cracking naphtha to premium gasoline
RNAA	=	Naphtha from type A crude to regular gasoline
RNAB	=	Naphtha from type B crude to regular gasoline
RNAC	=	Catalytic cracking naphtha to regular gasoline
FNAB	=	Naphtha from crude oil type B to fuel oil blend
FDIS	=	Distillate stocks to fuel oil blend
FRES	=	Residual stocks to fuel oil blend
FLCY	=	Light-cycle oil to fuel oil blend
FHCY	=	Heavy-cycle oil to fuel oil blend
CRAD	=	Type A crude oil processed for maximum distillate
CRAF	=	Type A crude oil processed for maximum fuel oil
CRBD	=	Type B crude oil processed for maximum distillate
CRBF	=	Type B crude oil processed for maximum fuel oil
CATD	=	Catalytic cracking distillate
CATL	=	Light-cycle oil recycled in catalytic cracking
CATH	=	Heavy-cycle oil recycled in catalytic cracking

(16), and (17) are octane number and RVP specifications for regular and premium gasoline. The coefficients of the *RRVP* equation have been arrived at as follows. [A similar procedure is followed for calculating the coefficients of the octane number and viscosity blending equation—equation (19).] The vapor pressures are given for all blending stocks in Table 4-8 and for the final products in Table 4-9. The maximum vapor pressure for premium gasoline (final products) should be 10. This means that blend stocks of premium gasoline, weighted by their respective vapor pressure, should be

$$(10)(PNAA + PNAB + PNAC) \geq (13)(PNAA) + (10)(PNAB) + (6)(PNAC)$$

The above inequalities can be rewritten as

$$0 \geq (13)(PNAA) - (10)(PNAA) + (10)(PNAB) - (10)(PNAB) + (6)(PNAC) - (10)(PNAC)$$

or

$$0 \geq (3)(PNAA) + (0)(PNAB) - (4)(PNAC)$$

The final equation is reflected in the linear programming matrix.

Table 4-12
Definition of Row Names (Constraints) in the Refinery Model

NAPA	=	Material balance for straight-run naphtha from crude type A for two modes of operation (fuel, distillate)
NAPB	=	Material balance for straight-run naphtha from crude type B for two modes of operation (fuel, distillate)
DIST	=	Material balance for straight-run distillate from crude types A and B
RESD	=	Material balance for residual fuel oil from crude types A and B
NAPC	=	Material balance for naphtha produced by catalytic cracking
CATL	=	Material balance of light-cycle oil generated by catalytic cracking
CATH	=	Material balance of heavy-cycle oil generated by catalytic cracking
CRDA	=	Upper limit on the availability of crude type A
CBAL	=	Equation for proportionate processing of crude types A and B
CCAP	=	Upper limit on the total quantity of crude oil charged to distillation unit
CATF	=	Catalytic cracking, recycling, and balance
RQUN	=	Blending equation on quantity of regular gasoline produced
ROCT	=	Blending equation on octane number of regular gasoline
RRVP	=	Blending equation on Reid vapor pressure of regular gasoline
PQUN	=	Blending equation on quantity of premium gasoline produced
POCT	=	Blending equation on octane number of premium gasoline produced
PRVP	=	Blending equation on Reid vapor pressure of premium gasoline
FQUN	=	Upper limit on production of fuel oil
FVIS	=	Blending equation of viscosity of fuel oil produced

Electricity Generation Models

The generation of electricity is another energy transformation component of the world energy model. The end product is electricity, and the inputs to be transformed are coal, natural gas, residual fuel oil, and nuclear fuel. Residual fuel oil is itself a product of refinery transformation, as described above. Natural gas, coal, and nuclear fuel, on the other hand, are energy resources that are supplied to electric power plants in their original, or primary, form. Synthetic fuels are not considered in the model.

The electricity sector in the world energy model is treated as follows. Initially, total demand for electricity is obtained by summing the demand for electricity in each demand sector. The conversion component of the model then satisfies this demand by selecting among different types of power plants including nuclear, hydroelectric, geothermal, and fossil fuel burning plants. Further, the world energy model allows for construction of new electric generation capacity by type of plant and whether such plants are to be used for base-load, cycling-load, or peak-load capacity. The selection among different types of power plants depends, among other things, upon the availability of fuels, costs of generating electricity, flexibility in switching input fuels, and overall plant efficiency. Thus, the world energy model determines how much fossil fuel (coal, residual fuel, natural gas, and distillate fuel) and nuclear fuel and capacity (existing and new) are required to satisfy the demand for electricity in different demand sectors.

The model operates by allocating to each region the appropriate generation capacity to meet electrical demand on the basis of minimum fuel plus generation cost. The price of electricity is defined as the average price to all consumers in each region.

The world energy model does not as yet include a detailed representation of electric power generation technology and associated economics for each region. In this sense, it differs from the refining model previously presented. A simplified structure is presented for electricity generation capacity and the fuel to be selected. Generation of electricity by nuclear, hydroelectric and geothermal plants is represented by regional vectors in the linear programming model which supply fixed amounts of electricity at fixed cost. Of course, the availability and selection of hydroelectric and geothermal capacity for a region are a function of geography. The selection of nuclear capacity is only for the base load and only for those regions which are both economically and technologically advanced. Electricity from fossil fuel plants is supplied on the basis of cost per kilowatt hour and involves use of appropriate quantities of coal, natural gas, or residual fuel oil. The construction of additional capacity by type of power plant is allowed in the model with corresponding capital investment expenditures.

The above procedure is mostly followed for all regions except the United States. A more detailed procedure is developed by PIES for the United States. It elaborates on the different parts of the electricity generation load duration curve: base-load, cycling-load, and peak-load capacities. Also it contains detailed technological representations of alternative electric generation plants.[10]

Logistic Models

Logistic activities are part of the supply side of the oil-importing countries' portion of the world energy model. These activities include the transportation of primary energy resources and final products among regions via various transportation modes. The cost of transportation depends upon the mode selected by the model. There is a constraint associated with the existing capacity for each mode of transportation. The model introduces new capacity requirements, however, if they are necessary to satisfy demand.

The importance of logistic network costs in the world energy model is not only that they are a component of energy prices, but also that fluctuations in transportation costs affect the liftings of crude oil from various countries. Thus, changes in transportation costs can be a source of conflict among OPEC countries and an important determinant of international energy flows and individual OPEC member country price and production policies. Finally, large sums of investment are involved in the transportation network and in the expansion of its capacity. The world energy model takes such interaction into account.

The logistic models in the world energy model include a detailed representation of the interregional movements of energy resources between each of the 20 regions depicted in Table 4-13. A total of 11 material-transport mode combinations are represented in the model:

1. Coal—rail
2. Coal—bulk carrier
3. Natural gas—LNG carrier
4. Natural gas—pipeline
5. Crude oil—small tanker
6. Crude oil—medium tanker
7. Crude oil—large tanker
8. Crude oil—VLCC
9. Crude oil—pipeline
10. Oil products—product tanker
11. Oil products—pipeline

The important physical or technological limitations which affect the distribution of energy are described within these transportation models. The capacities of the energy transportation systems are represented as upper limits on total shipments between regions. In addition, the expansion of these capacities is included as activities governing energy distribution, and the cost of this expansion is compared with the other alternatives available in the world energy model.

The eleven material-transportation modes listed above involve the use of different classes of shipping. Four size categories of oil tankers are specified in order to reflect the differing economies of the various-size tankers and to depict the physical restrictions of canal passage and port access. *Small tankers* are defined to be those that are capable of transit through the Panama and Suez Canals when fully laden with cargo. These would include most tankers below 55,000 dwt (deadweight tons) in size. *Medium tankers* are specified to be those too large for canal passage (when fully laden) but which are small enough for direct access to most ports throughout the world. These would include tankers between 55,000 and 70,000 dwt in size. *Large tankers*—those between 70,000 and 200,000 dwt—are those whose draft requirements prohibit their direct access to most United States, Canadian, and Mediterranean ports but which normally do not require the use of superports for access to other areas of the world. The fourth class, VLCC, includes all tankers above 200,000 dwt in size, which require the availability of superports to offload their cargo. It is assumed that both the medium- and large-size tankers can transit the Suez Canal whenever sailing in ballast. This routing significantly shortens the travel times of these tankers when returning to the Persian Gulf from their destinations in Europe and the Western Hemisphere.

Transportation Network

A separate transportation network is maintained in the model for each of the 11 material-transport mode pairs listed above. Each network is defined by a set of origin-destination pairs which constitute single arc routes between points of supply and points of consumption. Since shipping is the predominant mode of transportation in the world energy model, these points of origin and destination are referred to as ports and are primarily seaports. However, they can be any location at the end of a pipeline, rail, or sea route. A total of 45 seaports are provided for in the model. These seaports, along with the regions in which they are located, are listed in Table 4-13.

A total of ten interregional pipelines are modeled. They are listed in Table 4-14. These pipelines represent the major interregional pipelines that exist today. The number of pipelines included in the model can be expanded to reflect those now under construction and those that are planned for the future. One major example is the Sumed pipeline now being constructed across Egypt.

A very limited rail network is included in the model in order to depict the overland movements of coal within Europe and from the United States to Canada. Rail movements of coal are modeled between the following regions:

Table 4-13
World Energy Model Tanker Ports

Regions	Ports
United States (PADs 1 to 4)	New York Houston
United States (PAD 5)	Los Angeles Tacoma
North Slope	Valdez
Canada	Montreal Point Tupper Vancouver
Caribbean/Central America	Freeport, Bahamas St. Croix, Virgin Islands Kingston, Jamaica Pointe-a-Pierre, Trinidad
Venezuela	Puerto LaCruz
South America: other	Sao Sebastio, Brazil Quentero Bay, Chile
Northern Europe	Rotterdam, Netherlands Gothenburg, Sweden LeHarve, France Milford Haven, U.K. Bantry Bay, U.K.
Southern Europe	Genoa, Italy Ravenna, Italy Trieste, Italy Site, France Algeciras, Spain
North Africa	Arzew, Algeria Marsa El Brega, Libya
South Africa	Bonny, Nigeria Durban, South Africa
Iran	Kharg Island
Saudi Arabia	Ras Tanura
Middle East: other	Mina al Ahmadi, Kuwait Das Island, Abu Dhabi Sidon, Lebanon Eilat, Israel
Southwest Asia	Bombay, India
Southeast Asia	Pulum Bukon, Singapore
Indonesia	Santan
Oceania	Sydney, Australia
Japan	Yokohama Okinawa

Table 4-14
Pipeline Network in the World Energy Model

Origin	Destination	Type
Iraq	Lebanon	Crude oil
Saudi Arabia	Lebanon	Crude oil
Southern Europe	Northern Europe	Crude oil
Canada	United States (PADs 1 to 4)	Crude oil
Canada	United States (PAD 5)	Crude oil
Iran	Russia	Natural gas
Russia	Austria	Natural gas
Mexico	United States (PADs 1 to 4)	Natural gas
Afghanistan	Russia	Natural gas
United States (PADs 1 to 4)	United States (PAD 5)	Refined product

1. United States (PADs 1 to 4) to Canada
2. Northern Europe to Southern Europe
3. Soviet Bloc/China (Eastern Europe) to Northern Europe
4. Soviet Bloc/China (Eastern Europe) to Southern Europe

This rail network may need to be expanded in order to reflect additional interregional movements of coal if the role of this resource in international trade increases.

Transshipment

The size of oil tankers has grown significantly in recent years, and many new tankers have exceeded the reception capabilities of major ports. The average size of a seagoing tanker has more than doubled in the last ten years, while the expansion of port facilities has progressed at a much slower pace. This situation is a problem principally for the ports in North America and in Europe.

The economics of using the new, larger tankers for the long voyages from the Persian Gulf to Europe and to the east coast of North America have induced development of transshipment points to service these markets. The larger tankers are used to transport oil from the Persian Gulf (and elsewhere) to these transshipment points, and then smaller tankers are used to move the oil to its final ports of destination. Three such transshipment ports are included in the world energy model. These ports and the regions that they service are as follows:

Transshipment Port	*Region Serviced*
Bantry Bay, U.K.	Northern Europe
Point Tupper, Canada	Canada
Freeport, Bahamas	United States (PADs 1 to 4)

Energy Supply Models

This section presents supply models for oil and gas and for coal. The purpose of these models is to generate a range of supply possibilities and their associated costs. These supply curves will interface with the demand curves in an equilibrium market clearing environment.

The oil and gas supply model presented in this chapter is particularly applicable to those countries or supply regions in which oil and gas is a private, profit-oriented enterprise. This model was originally developed by the National Petroleum Council (NPC), and the results were used as inputs to the NPC *U.S. Energy Outlook*.[11] This model was later adopted by the FEA, modified, and used for generating inputs to Project Independence and the FEA's *1976 National Energy Outlook* report. The results of this model for the United States are used in the world energy model. A brief description of the model is presented in this chapter. A more detailed description may be found in the foregoing report. The supplies of oil and gas for the other OECD countries (except the United States) are based on the elasticities estimated from supply figures reported by OECD countries in *Energy Prospects to 1985*.[12] These estimates are presented in Chapter 5. The oil and gas supplies for developing countries (other than Communist Bloc and OPEC countries) are also based on estimated elasticities, and supplies for the Communist Bloc are treated as exogenous. The supplies for OPEC countries are presented in Part III.

The coal supply model is similar to the United States oil and gas supply model used by FEA. A brief description of this model is presented in this chapter. A more detailed description is found in the *1976 National Energy Outlook*. The model is applied to the United States. Coal supplies for all other countries, except the Communist Bloc, are estimated based on elasticities. Communist Bloc coal supplies are not considered.

Oil and Gas Supply Model

The oil and gas supply model for the United States is an engineering rather than an econometric representation of oil and gas production. The model determines the *minimum acceptable selling price* corresponding to a certain level of production. The minimum acceptable selling price covers costs plus a certain rate of return on investment. Thus, the supply curve generated is different from those generated based on marginal production decisions as functions of cost or price.

Generation of Supply Curves for Oil and Gas. Oil and gas supply curves for the United States are expressed as functions of minimum acceptable selling prices to producers. They are approximated by step functions in order to be compatible with the linear programming formulations of the supply side of the world energy model. Although the price-supply relationships for the other areas of the world (excluding OPEC) are estimated with use of elasticities or imposed exogenously rather than by developing minimum acceptable prices, they, too, are introduced into the world energy model as step functions. The step function supply curve of Figure 4-6 indicates that at a $4.00 price, 4 million bbl/D of oil will be produced and that at $8.00, the production increases from 4 to 10 million bbl/D. At $12, production increases from 10 to 14 million bbl/D. The lower steps of this curve could be interpreted as reflecting the use of cheaper (i.e., primary) methods of producing oil and gas, and the higher steps could be interpreted as reflecting the use of more expensive methods, such as secondary and tertiary recovery.

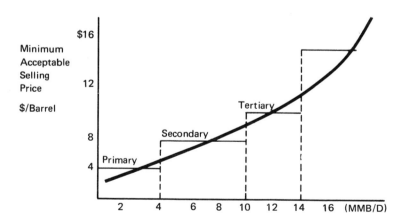

Figure 4-6. Crude Oil Supply Curve.

The model uses the following procedure to generate the oil and gas supply curves for the United States. Oil and gas supply activities are divided into exploration, development, and production activities. Exploration activities, including geological/geophysical work, leasing, and wildcatting, are performed on potential oil resources to determine the amount of oil in place. Development activities such as development drilling, producing wells, construction of substructure, and enhanced recoveries are then performed to translate the amount of oil in place into proved and recoverable reserves. Finally, production activities such as operating and maintaining producing wells are performed in order to bring oil to the surface and to optimally extract and deplete reserves. These activities are shown in Figure 4-7. Naturally, certain investment decisions

Figure 4-7. Integrated Oil and Gas Exploration and Production Analytical Sequence.

are associated with each of the above three major activities. These investment activities can be translated later to cost per unit of activity and, eventually, to a minimum acceptable selling price.

The following steps present a detailed procedure for determining cost- or price-sensitive supply curves for oil and gas. The following material is based on the description of the model by ICF, Inc. in support of the FEA PIES and the *National Energy Outlook* reports.

First, exploratory activities are translated into new oil in place. The finding rate (barrel per foot) is the major instrument for such a translation. The finding rate is measured by applying a statistical formulation to available exploratory or judgmental data (see Figure 4-8).

$$FR = Y_0 \cdot e^{-(Y_0/A)(FT)}$$

where Y_0 = Y intercept; represents an initial finding rate (bbl/ft)
   FR = finding rate (bbl/ft drilled)
   A = remaining discoverable resources (bbl)
   FT = cumulative exploratory footage drilled (ft)

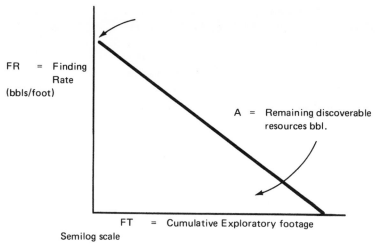

FR = Finding Rate (bbls/foot)

A = Remaining discoverable resources bbl.

FT = Cumulative Exploratory footage

Semilog scale

Figure 4-8. Finding Rate Curve.

Such a formulation indicates that the finding rate declines exponentially as cumulative exploratory activities (footage) increase. Of course, the parameters of the above equation vary for each world region.

The second step is to translate gradation in depths of resources into exploratory drilling expenditures. The cost per foot drilled is an increasing function of depth. (It also influences the finding rate to some extent.) The following relationships are used for estimation.

$$EXPW = (WD)(ADCF)$$

$$ADCF = f(WD)$$

$$WD = f(CEXFD)$$

where WD = well depth
$CEXFD$ = cumulative exploratory feet drilled
$ADCF$ = average drilling cost per foot
$EXPW$ = expenditure per well

Thus, expenditures per well are directly related to depth.

Third, oil in place is translated into proved or recoverable reserves. The recovery factor is an important instrument for such translation. Recovery factors are given not only for every region but also for each recovery method such as primary, secondary and tertiary. Next, the most profitable opportunities in any of the three primary, secondary, and tertiary recovery methods or any of their combinations at different levels of expected prices for crude oil are determined.

Fourth, the results of exploratory activities are translated into developmental drilling. The number of developmental wells drilled is representative of the intensity of development investment and the production rate. Thus, developmental feet drilled per barrel of oil in place discovered is the major determinant of investment decisions.

The fifth step is to translate reserve additions into production. The following equation establishes such a relationship for a single reservoir.

$$Q_t = \alpha \cdot R \cdot e^{-\alpha t}$$

where Q_t = production of oil
  α = decline rate (proxied by production/reserve ratios in latest years)
  R = proved reserve added

Sixth, the minimum acceptable price for each discrete investment decision is obtained by solving the following relationship for the price of oil (P_0).

$$I_e = \left\{ [(P_0 \cdot Q_e) + CR_e] (1 - Y) \right\} - C_e$$

$$- \left\{ [(P_0 \cdot Q_e) + CR_e] (1 - Y) - C_e - NC_e \right\} \cdot TR$$

where
  C_e = PVE annual cash expenditures
  NC_e = Annual noncash expenditures
  TR = marginal tax rate
  Y = joint ad valorem, severence, and royalty rate
  I_e = investment expenditures =capitalized investment $+(1 - TR)$ expense investment
  P_0 = price of oil
  Q_e = quantity of oil produced
  CR_e = annual revenue from nonoil hydrocarbon resources
  $\left[(P_0 \cdot Q_e + CR_e] (1 - Y) \right.$ = present value equivalent of annual revenues

Seventh, ultimate exploratory drilling is estimated as a function of price. The demand for drilling as a function of price represents gradation in the quality of prospects and is calculated by the model through numerous hypothetical exploratory drilling programs in all regions. Figure 4-9 shows that each region has a unique relationship between the demand for drilling and price. This figure shows cumulative exploratory drilling as related to price. The total demand for drilling at price P_1 is the horizontal summation of the exploratory drillings at that price. That is,

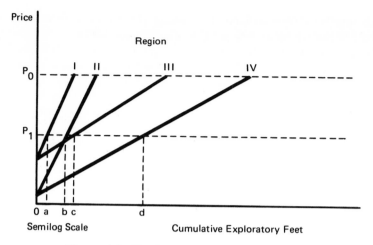

Figure 4-9. Exploratory Drilling Curve.

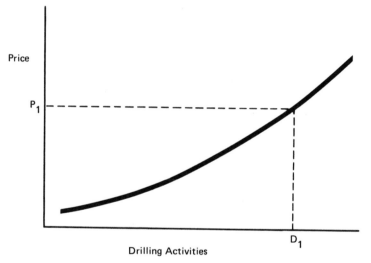

Figure 4-10. Drilling Activities Curve.

$$D_1 = 0a + 0b + 0c + 0d = \sum_j d_{1,j}$$

where j is the number of regions. This figure is drawn on semilog scale.

The eighth step is to allocate exploratory drilling over time. This is done by considering the economic life and capacity of rigs. Finally, the response of drilling to price is estimated. Figure 4-10 shows an oil price trajectory which implies a total demand for drilling. This trajectory is estimated through hypothetical drilling programs estimated earlier.

The price-sensitive drilling trajectories are drawn in Figure 4-11, based on the previous figure. This family of trajectories defines a supply curve for drilling subject to instantaneous, constant price trajectories.

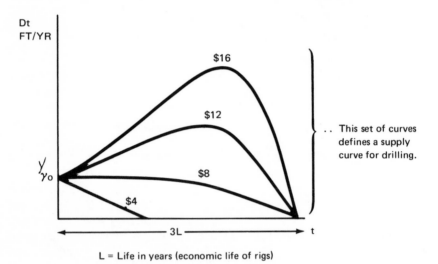

L = Life in years (economic life of rigs)

Figure 4-11. Drilling Trajectories.

In summary, the oil and gas supply model identifies a set of profitable total exploratory and development drilling opportunities at different levels of supply prices. These opportunities are limited at a given supply price since the size of discovered reservoirs becomes degraded as drilling activities are expanded. The yield (production) of crude oil and natural gas reserves over time is approximated as a declining function of cumulative footage drilled (degradation process).

The economics of drilling projects depends upon the rate of increase in costs and in the decrease in yield per foot as drilling activities progress. Thus, total drilling projects are identified, and the cumulative amount of drilling is estimated.

Once the cumulative amount of drilling for each relevant supply region is determined, an estimate of drilling activities over time is made using certain probable heuristic assumptions about the life of rigs and their operating conditions. This scheme produces a drilling rate allocation over time with an increase initially, a peak, and then a decline over a number of years.

Once the range of supply possibilities is generated, the total cost for each profile is calculated, using a discounted cash flow analysis for drilling and operating costs and assuming a certain real rate of return on investment. The entire process produces a different supply price, drilling, and production pattern for each reserve addition by year, region, and method of recovery. The total cost for each such increment is calculated individually to build an approximation to the cost curve. Thus, for each supply region, the total cost for each supply possibility is calculated.

Coal Supply Model

The purpose of the coal supply model is to generate price-sensitive supply curves for coal from new and existing surface and deep mines in each coal supply region for the United States. The quantity of coal produced is expressed as a function of increments in "minimum acceptable prices," which cover capital and operating costs plus a specified discounted cash flow (DCF) rate of return on investment. This approach is similar to one used for estimating oil and gas supply curves.

Among the numerous factors affecting the minimum acceptable selling price for coal are mining technology, operating conditions, productivity of labor and capital, supply of skilled labor, operating costs, and government regulations. Other factors, such as seam thickness and depth of the mine from the surface, are important for selecting between surface and underground mining.[14]

The following section describes a procedure for constructing coal supply curves.

Generation of Coal Supply Curves. Coal supply curves are generated for both surface and deep mines. The parameters of a surface mine are mine size and the overburden ratio; and the parameters of a deep mine are mine size, seam thickness, and seam depth. The production level of coal for each type of mine is based on the demonstrated reserve base. The coal supply curve methodology assigns the coal reserves to the various mine types and then translates the reserve stock into a flow of potential production, given an assumed mine life and assumed recovery factor. The price for each mine type is the minimum acceptable selling price, i.e., the minimum price that covers all operating costs, recovers the invested capital, and earns a specified return on invested capital. The following steps are taken in generating the coal supply curves.

First, the estimated coal reserves—by tonnage, quality characteristics, seam, and mining method—are obtained and assigned to coal supply regions, and within each region assigned to product classes. Three product classes are recognized: metallurgical coal, low-sulfur coal, and high-sulfur coal.[15]

Second, the production of existing coal mines is estimated, and reserves committed to these mines are eliminated from the total reserves available. Existing capacity is treated separately because the capital investment is sunk. Only the operating costs are relevant in considering the marginal cost of coal from existing capacity (i.e., the mine would continue producing as long as prices are high enough to cover variable costs). This is not to say that only operating costs are included in the actual prices.

Third, the uncommitted strippable coal reserves are allocated to overburden-ratio categories, since the overburden ratio of a coal seam appears to be a major factor in determining the cost of strip-mining the coal.[16] It is assumed that the highest overburden ratio would be 45:1 for bituminous coal and 20:1 for subbituminous coal and lignite.

Fourth, the uncommitted deep coal reserves are allocated to seam thickness and depth categories. The thickness and depth of coal seams appear to be major determinants of the costs of deep mining. The methodology used to assign reserves to seam thickness categories is similar to that used to assign reserves to overburden-ratio categories.

Fifth, the uncommitted reserves are also allocated to mine-size categories. For strippable reserves, the maximum mine size is based upon maximum size strip-mines being planned within a region between now and 1985. For deep-mine reserves, the number of mine size categories is dependent upon the seam thickness.

Sixth, the production estimates are assigned to mine types. The first few steps of the coal supply curve methodology break the estimated reserves data into smaller and smaller categories. The strippable coal reserves are broken down by region, coal type, overburden ratio, and mine size. The deep coal reserves are broken down by region, coal type, seam thickness, seam depth, and mine size. This step in the methodology translates these disaggregated reserve categories into annual production potential by mine types. Recovery factors of 0.6 for deep mines and 0.8 for surface mines are assumed. The life of a mine is assumed to be 30 years.

Seventh, estimates of minimum acceptable selling prices for each mine type per ton of coal are obtained. This is accomplished by establishing two "base-case" mine-cost models, one strip mine and one deep mine, and a matrix of adjustment factors for costing changes in key variables.

Finally, mine types with associated production levels are arranged in order of minimum acceptable selling prices. The price is used to collapse 30 years of inflating minimum acceptable selling prices into a single value, for potential coal production for the same mine type, coal type, and region. The mine types for each supply curve are then arranged in order of increasing price. These supply possibilities are in step-function form with the lower steps representing the coal produced from lower-cost mines (e.g., existing surface mines and higher steps representing the coal produced from higher-cost mines). This implies that coal from cheaper mines is produced first in meeting the demand of consumers and that of the most expensive mines is produced last. Figure 4-12 represents a sample of such coal supply possibilities. Thus, each step of the supply curve reflects the quantity of coal which will be produced at different price levels. The production level associated with each step is the maximum annual production that the reserve base could sustain from that particular mine for 30 years.

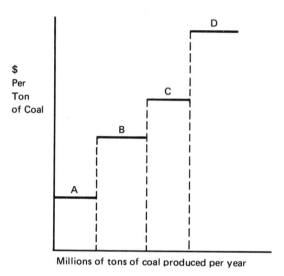

A = Existing surface mines
B = Existing deep mines
C = New surface mines
D = New deep mines

Figure 4-12. Coal Supply Curve.

Integrating Framework of the World Energy Model

The world energy model (oil-importing countries) is a one-period equilibrium, multisectoral, econometric-linear programming model. In a true sense, it consists of several submodels (described earlier in this chapter), which are brought together through an integrating framework. The demand curve for each final energy product, the supply curve for each primary energy resource, and the supply technology for transforming and transporting energy among regions, generated by the above submodels, are used in the integrating framework to determine equilibrium prices and quantities of all forms of energy simultaneously. The mathematical structure of the integrating framework consists of a demand-side, supply-side (i.e., the technology of energy transformation and transportation), and an equilibrium solution algorithm. The demand side is represented by an econometric structure and the supply side by a linear programming structure.

Demand-Side Structure

The demand curve for each final energy product for each region is expressed as a function of the price of the product, prices of competing energy products, and other major economic variables. These relationships were estimated by econometric techniques and explained in detail under the energy demand model earlier in this chapter. These demand curves are approximated by a step function, where each step represents an increment (decrement) in price and quantity. The generalized form of the approximated demand curve is presented in Figure 4-13.

The general form of the demand function $Q(P)$ is written as

$$Q_0 = Q(P_0)$$

P_0 represents the set of energy prices and Q_0 the set of quantities for the same forms of energy. Then, using the implied own-price elasticities, an approximate price function with zero cross elasticities can be constructed such that

$$P_0 = P_d(Q_0)$$

This relationship shows that for every increment (or decrement) in the price of a final energy product and in the prices of competing products, a decrement (or increment) in the quantity of that particular energy product can be determined.

Supply-Side Structure

The supply of each primary form of energy in each region is also represented by a price-sensitive supply curve, which is approximated by a step function (see Figure 4-14). These curves are constructed by energy supply models presented earlier in this chapter.

In order to meet final energy demands, primary energy supplies are transported and transformed into final products. The technology of these

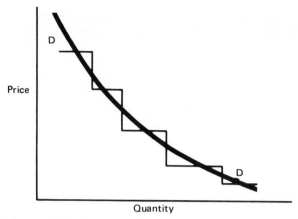

Figure 4-13. Demand Curve and Its Approximation.

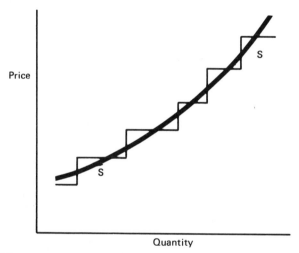

Figure 4-14. Supply Curve and Its Approximation.

supply activities is presented through a series of linear relationships or constraints.

The supply-side structure has the following types of constraints. Each of them is described briefly below.

1. Supply balances
2. Demand balances
3. Conversion balances
4. Material balances
5. Crude attribute balances
6. Refining capacity constraints
7. Arc traffic constraints
8. Transport mode traffic balance
9. Vehicle availability constraints
10. Port throughput constraints
11. Capital requirements balances

In addition, other constraints can be included in the model as required.

The supply and demand balances aggregate the detailed country-level supply and demand quantities and ensure that they are equal to world totals.

The conversion balances serve the same purpose as those for supply and demand except that the quantities collected are for those materials (except for refined petroleum products) which are converted or transformed prior to being supplied as final products. The primary example of this is the transformation of coal, natural gas, and fuel oil into electricity.

The material balance constraints ensure that the quantity of any given resource or product consumed in a region does not exceed the quantity of that resource either which is supplied from within the region or which has been transported to the region for consumption.

In order to reflect the dynamics of refinery operations in the processing of different crude oils, a number of properties of each type of crude are tracked explicitly in the model through crude attribute balances. Two different crude oils will, in general, produce a significantly different mix of products when they are processed through any given refinery. In order to adequately address this problem, the model is designed to select crude oils for a refinery in such a way that feasible balances of up to ten different crude attributes are maintained.

The refining capacity constraints restrict the use of refineries of each region to be the capacity that is currently available plus the capacity that can be constructed under the applicable constraints on time, capital expenditures, and investment.

The arc traffic constraints and the transport mode traffic constraints serve as a means of measuring the total traffic over each origin-destination pair, by mode by transportation, and the total traffic generated across all arcs for each such mode. The arc traffic constraints also serve as a means of constraining the flow over any arc because of throughput constraints such as pipeline capacity or other restrictions.

Other constraints that could affect the flow of transportation are vehicle availability and port throughput. The utilization of vehicles is restricted to the use of the current fleet of tanker and bulk ships less anticipated scrappage plus the number of new ships built under the applicable time, capital, and return-on-investment requirements.

The capital requirement balances require that the total capital expended within each region of the world be warranted on a cost/benefit basis using a return-on-investment rate that is deemed appropriate for that region. This mechanism makes it possible to reflect regional differences in the availability of capital for energy purposes as well as alternative risk factors associated with making the required investment. Capital may be available in one region for long-term investment and thus require low rates of return, whereas in another region the limited amounts of capital available are needed only for short-term projects with a resultant high rate of return on investment.

The preceding constraints can be categorized into two groups: activity constraints and capacity constraints. The formal mathematical exposition of the constraints is presented below in terms of these two groups and is followed by the formulation for the objective function. The general exposition and notations of these relationships follow closely the PIES framework by William W. Hogan.[17]

Acitivity Constraints. The relationships below explain the major supply activities in the world energy market, such as production, transportation, and transformation. The activities are defined as follows:

$S_{i,l}$ = production of product increment i in region l

$T_{i,l,k,m}$ = transportation of energy product i from region l to region k via transportation mode m

$R_{l,n}$ = refining, processing, and other transformation of energy by plant n in region l

These activities encounter a number of physical restrictions, or limits, which are presented below.

The first group of constraints in the supply model establishes bounds for each increment in production activity. It should be recalled that the supply curve for each form of energy is approximated by a step function. These constraints ensure that the quantity of any particular form of energy delivered to the transportation sector does not exceed the available supply.

The bound for the production activity is denoted by $BS_{i,l}$. (The B preceding the variable stands for bound.)

$$0 \leq S_{i,l} \leq BS_{i,l}$$

Of course, the supply of different energy forms is a function of reserves, price and location of the raw material, etc.

The transportation sector is characterized by the nature and size of the mode of transport in addition to the loading (producing) and unloading (demand) locations. The transportation activities are represented by the following type of equations with the boundary value of $BT_{i,l,k,m}$.

$$0 \leq T_{i,l,k,m,} \leq BT_{i,l,k,m}$$

It is assumed that no loss occurs during transportation. It is further required that transportation capacity be at least sufficient to transport the necessary amount of $S_{i,l}$.

The transformation capacities and activities are represented by

$$0 \le R_{l,n} \le BR_{l,n}$$

The material balance of each region and each form of energy should be established. That is, the amount of each form of energy transported to outside a region should be less than or equal to total production of that form within the region.

$$-S_{i,l} + \sum_{m} \sum_{k} T_{i,l,k,m} \le 0$$

Similarly, the material balance for the transformation, including refining, regions should be established. The technologies of transformation are represented by

$$\sum_{m} \sum_{k} T_{i,l,k,m} - \sum_{m} \sum_{k} T_{i,k,l,m} - \sum_{i} r_{i,n} \cdot R_{l,n} \le 0$$

where $r_{i,n}$ is the input ($r_{i,n} < 0$) or output ($r_{i,n} > 0$) of product (i) per unit of activity of plant (n).

Capacity Constraints. Production, transportation, refining, and other conversion facilities have potential capacity limitations. The levels of these activities should be equal to or less than the capacities available. In many cases, the model has the capability to build additional facilities and capacities as it becomes necessary.

The transportation network is limited by the availability and mode of transportation. The upper-bound capacity constraint is shown by $UT_{l,k,m}$.

$$\sum_{i} T_{i,l,k,m} \le UT_{l,k,m}$$

The refining and other transformation constraints ensure that the existing capacity is greater than or equal to the levels of the related activities.

$$\sum_{n} R_{l,n} \le UR_{l}$$

The above relationships are supplemented by limitations on the availability of key complementary resources (e.g., manpower, steel, etc.). If $s_{i,l,q}$, $t_{i,l,k,m,q}$, and $r_{l,n,q}$, represent the requirements for a resource (q) per unit of production, transportation, or conversion, then the aggregate constraint on availability of the cross-cut resource can be limited to the value (UC_q) via the inequality

$$\sum_{i} \sum_{l} s_{i,l,q} \cdot S_{i,l} + \sum_{i} \sum_{l} \sum_{k} \sum_{m}$$

$$t_{i,l,k,m,q} \cdot T_{i,l,k,m} + \sum_{l} \sum_{n} r_{l,n,q} \cdot R_{l,q} \leq UC_q$$

The above constraints are combined with the demand equations and represented as

$$\sum_{l} \sum_{m} T_{i,l,k,m} = D_{i,k}$$

where $D_{i,k}$ is the demand for the ith product in the kth region.

The Objective Function. The objective function of the linear programming supply model is presented below. Its coefficients ($s_{i,l,o}$, $t_{i,l,k,m,o}$, and $r_{l,n,o}$) represent the minimum acceptable price for each unit of activity.

$$\min \sum_{i} \sum_{l} s_{i,l,o} \cdot S_{i,l} + \sum_{i} \sum_{l} \sum_{k} \sum_{m}$$

$$t_{i,l,k,m,o} \cdot T_{i,l,k,m} + \sum_{l} \sum_{q} r_{l,n,o} \cdot R_{l,n}$$

Equilibrium Solution Algorithm

The equilibrium algorithm integrates the supply and demand functions to arrive at equilibrium prices, demand, supply, imports, exports, and flows through an iterative procedure.

The world energy model (oil-importing countries) is designed to simulate equilibrium energy prices, supply, and demand for each region of the world. For each region, a level of demand and corresponding price are determined for each end product consistent with its price elasticities and the resultant costs of providing that product in the region. The *equilibrium price* of a product in a region is defined to be the price at which the quantities supplied and demanded are equal.

The following simple example demonstrates the basic reasoning used in the equilibrium solution algorithm. Suppose that one is interested in determining the equilibrium quantity and price for the supply and demand curves shown in Figure 4-15. In order to use optimization theory in solving this problem, one could make use of the fact that the equilibrium combination of quantity and price is that quantity which maximizes the difference between the area under the demand curve to the left of this quantity and the similar area under the supply curve. This difference, the sum of the producers' and consumers' surplus, is referred to as *surplus* in this example. The intersection of supply and demand curves is obtained by finding the quantity and price which maximize the surplus.[18]

In order to solve the above problem with linear programming, the supply and demand curves should be approximated by step functions as presented in Figure 4-16. S_i is the amount of supply available at marginal cost C_i, and D_j is the amount of demand available at price P_j. Supply and demand curves are often computed in just such a stepwise fashion by disaggregating sources and markets, so such an "approximation" is often wholly natural. More importantly, it makes it possible to use linear programming to solve the problem.

If the demand curves are represented in J steps and supply curves in I steps, then one can define the nonnegative quantity variables X_i ($i = 1, 2, \ldots, I$) and Y_j ($j = 1, 2, \ldots, j$) and consider the linear program

$$\max Z = \sum_{j=1}^{J} P_j Y_j - \sum_{i=1}^{I} C_i X_i$$

$$\text{subject to } \sum_{i=1}^{I} X_i - \sum_{j=1}^{J} Y_j = 0$$

$$0 \leq X_i \leq S_i \qquad i = 1, 2, \ldots, I$$
$$0 \leq Y_j \leq D_j \qquad j = 1, 2, \ldots, J$$

It is obvious that the solution to this problem will maximize the surplus, since the linear program will automatically use up the high-value demands and low-cost supplies. The program merely restates the problem as one of maximizing the area under the demand curve less the area under the supply curve subject to the constraint that supply equals demand. X_i is the amount of the ith supply category actually produced, and Y_j is the amount of the jth demand category actually supplied. The equilibrium quantity is equal to $\sum X_i$ or $\sum Y_j$.

Ordinarily this will be an inefficient way to solve the above problem as compared to the usual process of equating supply and demand and simultaneously solving the equations. However, the linear programming

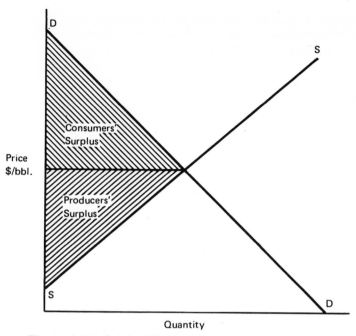

Figure 4-15. Original Demand and Supply Curves.

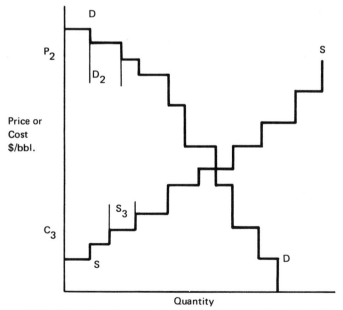

Figure 4-16. Stepwise Approximation to Demand and Supply Curves.

method leads to a straightforward solution algorithm for which the usual method of solving a large set of simultaneous nonlinear equations will often prove computationally infeasible.

Given this possibility of generalization, it is of interest to examine the dual of the above problem. Let W be the dual variable associated with the equilibrium constraint; let U_i $(i = 1, 2, \ldots, I)$ be the variable associated with the supply constraints; and let V_j be the variable associated with the demand constraints. Then, the dual of the linear programming problem is

$$\min Z' = \sum_{j=1}^{J} D_j V_j + \sum_{i=1}^{I} S_i U_i$$

Subject to:
$$V_j + W \geq P_j \quad j = 1, 2, \ldots, J$$
$$U_i - W \geq -C_i \quad i = 1, 2, \ldots, I$$

Using complementary slackness, if $X_j \leq D_j$ is actually limiting, equality holds in the dual and $V_j + W = P_j$ or $V_j = P_j - W$. W is the equilibrium price, and V_j is the difference in the amount that people in the jth sector would be willing to pay and the price (the unit net benefit to this group). Similarly, for those supply sectors actually used, U_i is the unit profit to these suppliers. Thus, at optimality, the first summation in the dual objective function is the consumers' surplus; the second is the producers' surplus. The dual solves the problem in an interesting way. For any given price W, any horizontal line in Figure 4-16 the dual minimizes the sum of the area above that line and below the demand curve and the area below that line and above the supply curve. The equilibrium price minimizes this sum over all W since it is the only price that includes no area to the right of either the supply curve or the demand curve.

Market simulation is effected by separating the supply and demand components, approximating the supply side, and then adjusting the prices and demands until the system achieves an equilibrium balance. Simulation of the supply side is achieved by assuming that, for a given set of prices, demands, and resource capacities, the energy supply system will operate to satisfy demand in a least-cost manner.

For an arbitrary selection of prices and demands, the least-cost balancing solution may not be an equilibrium solution; there is no means of guaranteeing that an arbitrary price for estimating product demand will be equal to the price at which the product is supplied. However, the dual variables associated with the demand constraints in the linear program identify the necessary adjustments in the prices, and these adjustments are repeated until the equilibrium solution is obtained.[19]

In order to compute the equilibrium prices for end products in a region, it is necessary to have the corresponding price-sensitive demand data. These data are made available to the model in the form of initial estimates of prices and quantities and a matrix of the product's own and cross elasticities with respect to price. Whenever these data are not available for a particular product or for all products within a particular region a single fixed price and quantity are imposed. The imposition of fixed demands and prices in the world energy model is to a large extent for those refined products with relatively small demands such as bitumen, paraffin waxes, lubricants, and other products.

5

Input Parameters and World Demand for OPEC Oil

This chapter presents and discusses some of the estimated coefficients, other input parameters, and assumptions used in the world energy model (oil-importing countries) developed in the preceding chapter. Selected results generated by this part of the model are also presented. Limited space precludes presentation of all such data. Some important historical trends of major indicators are also presented.

Ideally, the world energy model should always use formally estimated parameters to represent energy markets in each of the various geographic regions. However, formal estimation of all coefficients of the model is not possible because of inadequate data, absence of market-oriented energy markets in certain regions, etc. Thus, some shortcuts had to be taken and professional judgment frequently had to be made in order to arrive at the necessary coefficients and other input parameters. In general, they were derived from a combination of formal estimation, estimates published in the literature, and judgment.

Estimated coefficients, other parameters, and assumptions for various components of the world energy model are discussed in the following sequence.

1. Demand
2. Refining and other energy conversion
3. Transportation
4. Supply

Demand Parameters

Empirical econometric studies for measuring demand for energy products in industrialized countries are limited and for developing countries are almost unavailable. However, many empirical studies have estimated United States energy demand. In particular, the Federal Energy Administration has constructed a simulation model to generate energy demand forecasts and elasticities for the United States. These elasticities are dependent on time and on levels of crude oil prices. The elasticities generated by FEA are for various energy scenarios, including one (the reference case) which represents the most likely future development of the United States energy economy if no special energy measures are adopted in future years. This particular scenario assumes that the landed price of imported oil into the United States will be $13.00 per barrel (in constant 1975 U.S. dollars) to 1985, or about $11.00 per barrel of crude oil f.o.b. Persian Gulf.

Tables 5-1 and 5-2 present selected price elasticities for final energy products in different end-use markets for the 1985 reference case. Table 5-1 presents elasticities for residential/commercial and industrial sectors. The mnemonic names at the top and side of the table represent different product names by sector. The diagonal elements in the table represent own-price elasticities, and the off-diagonal elements in the table represent cross elasticities. The mnemonic names in the tables can be interpreted as follows. The first two characters represent the type of energy form, and the third and fourth characters are used to identify a particular sector. Table 5-2 presents price elasticities for energy products in the transportation sector. The elasticities in both tables are used as inputs to the world energy model to estimate the United States demand for energy.

The price and income elasticities of demand generated by the Adams-Griffin model for the OECD countries (excluding the United States) for all energy forms are used as inputs to the world energy model.[1] For illustration, some of the price elasticities are presented in Table 5-3.

Primary energy consumptions actually used as inputs to the world energy model were the most recent data available at the time the model was solved. The consumption data presented in Table 5-4 are for the latest year (1975) available at the time of writing.

Refining and Other Energy Conversion Parameters

The refining industry of each refining region is represented by a composite refinery model derived by aggregating the process units (by types) of all the refineries in that region. The relationships between units and operations are formulated mathematically through linear programming. These models select a least-cost method of converting crude oil to finished products by either utilizing existing facilities or constructing new plants. Alternative solutions of these models under various assumptions are then abstracted and used as possible modes of operation in the world energy model.[2] A mode (or an extreme point) consists of aggregate product yields, aggregate crude volume and characteristics, operating, and investment cost. The world energy model selects any combination of these modes which satisfies the objective function. These modes of operation are generated by the Refinery and Petrochemical Modeling System (RPMS).[3]

Table 5-1
Price Elasticities for Energy Products for Selected United States Energy Sectors

	Household/Commercial Sector					
	ELHC	NGHC	DFHC	RFHC	KSHC	LGHC
ELHC	−.510	.075	.054	−.007	.011	.058
NGHC	.260	−.721	.024	.017	.008	.042
DFHC	.252	.063	−.750	.007	.001	.018
RFHC	.278	−.020	.018	−.594	−.002	−.002
KSHC	.178	.053	.056	.000	−.778	.046
LGHC	.079	.017	.025	.000	.001	−.567

	Industrial Sector						
	ELIN	NGIN	DFIN	RFIN	KSIN	LGIN	BCIN
ELIN	−.469	.062	.048	.049	.009	.028	.029
NGIN	.119	−.392	.010	.007	.001	.005	.006
DFIN	.213	.108	−.701	.028	.002	.009	.013
RFIN	.075	.049	−.006	−.416	−.002	−.006	−.002
KSIN	.223	.093	.020	.034	−.721	.008	.015
LGIN	.195	.138	.017	.024	.002	−.715	.010
BCIN	.225	.084	.017	.020	.001	.006	−.562

Note: The characters in mnemonic names are defined as follows. First two characters:

EL: Electricity
NG: Natural gas
DF: Distillate fuel
RF: Residual fuel
KS: Kerosene
LG: Liquid gases
BC: Bituminous coal (fuel and power)

Third and fourth characters:

HC: Household/Commercial sector
IN: Industrial sector

Source: *1976 National Energy Outlook,* Federal Energy Administration, February 1976, Washington, D.C.

Table 5-2

Price Elasticities for Energy Products for the United States Transportation Sector

Automobile vehicle miles	-.480
Airline passenger miles	-.245
Truck fuel demand	-.545
Bus fuel demand	-.475
Rail diesel fuel demand	-.368

Source: *1976 National Energy Outlook,* Federal Energy Administration, February 1976, Washington, D.C.

Table 5-3

Price Elasticities for Energy Products for Selected OECD Energy Sectors

	Transportation Sector		
Fuel Type	Coal	Heavy Fuel Oil	Light Fuel Oil
Coal	−1.04	0.85	0.17
Heavy fuel oil	−0.03	0.34	0.55
Light fuel oil	−0.09	−0.07	−0.10
Electricity	1.11	−0.15	0.25
LPG	−1.03	−1.02	−1.03

	Residential Sector			
	Coal	Gas	Kerosene	Light Fuel Oil
Coal	−0.81	−0.62	0.81	−0.35
Gas	0.82	−1.05	−0.54	0.98
Kerosene	0.39	0.11	−0.57	0.44
Light fuel oil	0.37	0.63	0.28	−0.33
LPG	0.10	1.85	−1.21	1.90

Table 5-3 (Continued)   *Iron and Steel Industry Sector*

	Coal	Gas	Heavy Fuel Oil	Electricity
Coal	−0.05	0.26	0.31	−0.31
Gas	−0.17	−0.17	0.72	0.19
Heavy fuel oil	−0.34	−0.37	−1.07	0.70
Electricity	0.98	0.26	0.26	−0.71

Other Industrial Sectors

	Coal	Gas	Heavy Fuel Oil	Electricity
Coal	−0.55	−0.22	0.75	−0.16
Gas	−0.03	−0.55	−0.41	1.73
Heavy fuel oil	−0.29	0.32	−0.26	−0.30
Electricity	0.13	0.11	−0.13	−0.28
LPG	−0.85	0.22	−0.73	1.51

Source: F. Gerard Adams and James M. Griffin, "Energy and Fuel Substitution Elasticities: Results from an International Cross-Section Study," Mimeo, University of Pennsylvania, August 1974.

Table 5-4
1975 World Energy Consumption
(millions of tons of oil equivalent)

	Oil	Natural Gas	Solid Fuels	Hydro	Nuclear	Total
United States	764.2	515.7	342.1	78.4	40.0	1740.4
Other OECD	1010.1	209.7	347.7	177.8	35.2	1780.5
Non-OECD Non-OPEC countries	325.30	57.5	232.9	54.3	1.5	671.5
OPEC	92.7	38.5	5.9	8.8	—	145.9
World (excluding Communist Bloc)	2193.3	821.4	928.6	319.3	76.7	4338.3

Source: The British Petroleum Company, Ltd., "BP Statistical Review of the World Oil Industry, 1975," London, 1976, and author's estimates.

Expected variations in refinery operations are explored with these refinery linear programming models and are based on judgments concerning regional refining capacity growth, future marginal crude supplies, and demand for petroleum products. Bounds on refining capacity were determined by analyzing announced refinery construction plans through 1980 and extrapolating at a reduced rate through 1985. Marginal supplies of crude in the United States case were considered by analyzing preliminary Project Independence Oil Task Force estimates of oil production. Demand variation was estimated from various (PIES) simulations.

The refinery and petrochemical modeling system (RPMS) used to formulate aggregate regional refinery models has the capability to generate linear programming matrices and data bases. The RPMS data base includes major world crude assays, process yield correlations, worldwide refinery capacity and configuration data, and investment and operating cost data which were used as the foundation for constructing the regional refinery models. The world crudes are presented through a set of representative crudes. Each of these crudes is derived by aggregating several crudes or selecting an individual crude from the RPMS crude assay library. A sample crude assay for Arabian Light 34° API is presented in Table 5-5.

The RPMS investment data used represent mid-year (1972) Gulf Coast construction cost information for each type of refinery processing unit, as well as associated expenses. Onsite investment costs include, in addition to process unit fabrication and assembly costs, the costs of necessary control houses, instrumentation, and site preparation. Offsite expenses include, in addition to process unit fabrication and assembly costs, the costs of necessary control houses, instrumentation, and site preparation. Offsite expenses include intermediate tankage, lines, etc., but do not include necessary utilities (steam plant, power plant, cooling towers, etc.), which are explicitly represented as separate processing units in the model. However, any costs resulting from initial site preparation (clearing and landscaping, office building, plant security, etc.) are excluded, as are costs of finished products or tankage.

A widely practiced method of comparing construction costs of refineries at various world regions is by use of so-called location factors. The refineries in the United States Gulf Coast have the lowest construction costs in the United States, and the costs of constructing refineries in various parts of the world are determined by applying escalation factors for these areas to the United States Gulf Coast costs.

Location factors exist for all refineries at all locations and vary substantially. Location factors for 1971-72 are presented in Table 5-6 relative to the United States Gulf Coast, which equals 1.00.

Table 5-5
Sample Crude Oil Assay Data (Arabian Light 34° API)

Distillation Fraction	API Gravity	Yield (wt %)	ASTM 50%	Octane Number (Motor)	Aromatic (Vol. %)	Naphtene (Vol. %)
57-155°F	9.859	4.73	118	69	0.4	2.4
155-310°F	8.836	12.13	234	43	9.6	20.4
310-375°F	8.229	5.84	337		17.2	23.3
375-500°F	7.946	11.77				
500-680°F	7.491	17.85				
680-800°F	7.165	12.25				
800-1000°F	6.741	17.57				
1000 +°F	6.275	16.65				

Distillation Fraction	Aniline Point	Vapor Pressure	Viscosity	Pour Point	Nickel and Vanadium (PPM)	Nitrogen (PPM)	Sulfur (wt %)
57-155°F	179	11.2					
155-310°F	135	1.6					
310-375°F	130	0.11					
375-500°F	142.8		30.9	-43.0		0.000183	0.266
500-680°F	155.0		38.7	21.0		0.007593	1.299
680-800°F	166.6		155.9	75.0		0.054263	1.939
800-1000°F			624.5	100.0			2.605
1000 +°F					121.0		4.040

Source: *Oil and Gas Journal,* RPMS, and author's estimates.

Table 5-6
Recommended Location Factors (1971-1972) Relative to the United States Gulf Coast

Location	Factor	Location	Factor
Gulf Coast, U.S. (Base)	1.00	Norway	0.96
California	1.09	Spain	0.86
East Coast	1.25	United Kingdom	0.89
Great Lakes	1.12	Average Europe	0.89
Louisiana	1.085	Australia	0.96
U.S., Average	1.066	Indonesia	0.90
Alaska, U.S. Equip.	1.35	Philippines	0.87
Eastern Canada	1.06	Average South Pacific	0.86
Average Canada	1.035	India, Eur. Equip.	0.95
		Jap. Equip.	0.87
Bahamas, U.S. Equip.	0.94		
Eur. Equip.	0.98	Average, Central Asia	0.93
Jap. Equip.	0.96	Iran, Eur. Equip.	0.97
Mexico, U.S. Equip.	0.94	Jap. Equip.	0.91
Venezuela, U.S. Equip.	1.03	Iraq	1.02
Eur. Equip.	0.99	Kuwait, U.S. Equip.	0.99
Jap. Equip.	0.96	Jap. Equip.	0.94
Average Caribbean	0.94	Average, Middle East	0.97
Brazil, U.S. Equip.	0.97	Japan	0.80
Eur. Equip.	0.93		
		Average Central Asia	0.93
France	0.88	Libya	1.28
Germany	0.91	S. Africa, Eur. Equip.	0.94
Italy	0.82	Jap. Equip.	0.90

Source: W.L. Nelson, "Refining Costs Compared throughout the World," *Oil and Gas Journal,* April 26, 1976.

The refinery construction cost components of the world energy model data base are adjusted by escalating the 1971-72 United States Gulf Coast data by 51 percent to reflect January 1, 1975 estimated costs in that area. Location factors for various world regions were then applied to adjust for regional costs differences. The following table summarizes some of these data.[4]

Investment Escalation Factors

United States Gulf Coast	(Base) 1.51
United States East Coast	1.84
United States Great Lakes	1.65
Wyoming	1.56
United States West Coast	1.63
Canada	1.60
Caribbean	1.42
Northern Europe	1.33
Southern Europe	1.27
Japan	1.13

These data were obtained from the literature, contractors, or calculated by W. L. Nelson. (A selection of even more recent data published by Nelson is found in the source cited in the footnote.[5])

Historical refining capacity is an input into the world energy model. The latest data available at the time that the model was simulated were used. Table 5-7 presents data (for 1975) which have since become available. Historical refinery yield patterns of petroleum products for 1975 are presented in Table 5-8. It is clear that the refinery yields in various geographic regions vary. For instance, a typical product mix for North America is to produce 46 percent gasoline, 29 percent middle distillate, 9 percent fuel oil, and 16 percent other products and waste. This product mix costs roughly $1.00 per barrel to produce. European slates in 1975 typically cost $0.35 per barrel and consisted of 21, 33, 33, and 13 percent for gasoline, middle distillate, fuel oil and other products respectively.

Transportation Parameters

Transportation costs associated with tanker movements are calculated on the basis of the average of current long-term charter and spot rates and are called *average freight rate assessment* (or AFRA) rates.[6] The rates are determined for each size category of tanker and are compiled monthly by the Association of Ship Brokers and Agents. The rates are expressed as a percentage of a set of reference freight rates called "world scale."[7] They are compiled by the same association and published periodically. Thus, an AFRA rate of 75 for a given size tanker is interpreted to mean that the average freight rate being charged is 75 percent of the reference rates over all trade routes for that size tanker.

Table 5-7
World Oil Refining Capacities at the End of 1975

Country/Area	1000 bbl/D, 1975[a]
United States	15,345
Canada	2215
Total North America	17,560
Latin America	
Argentina	725
Brazil	1020
Mexico	735
N.W.I.	900
Trinidad	460
Venezuela	1500
Other Latin America	2290
Total Latin America	7630
Total Western Hemisphere	25,190
Western Europe	
Belgium	975
France	3510
Italy	4405
Netherlands	1950
Spain	1180
United Kingdom	2950
West Germany	3115
Other Western Europe	2835
Total Western Europe	20,920
Middle East	
Aden	160
Bahrain	250
Iran	765
Iraq	185
Kuwait	565
Neutral Zone	75
Saudi Arabia	465
Other Middle East	335
Total Middle East	2800
Africa	1240
South Asia	720
Southeast Asia	
Indonesia	415
Singapore	1095
Other Southeast Asia	1380
Total Southeast Asia	2890
Japan	5345
Australia	765

Table 5-7 (Continued)

U.S.S.R., Eastern Europe, and China	12,250
Total Eastern Hemisphere	46,930
World	72,120
World (excluding U.S.S.R., Eastern Europe, and China)	59,870

[a]Per calendar day.

Source: British Petroleum Company, Ltd., "BP Statistical Review of the World Oil Industry 1975," 1976.

Table 5-8
Percentage Refinery Yields on Crude Oil in 1975

Area and Products	Percentage Yield by Volume
North America	
Gasoline	46
Middle distillates	29
Fuel oil	9
Other products[a]	16
Western Europe	
Gasoline	21
Middle distillate	33
Fuel oil	33
Other products[a]	13
Japan	
Gasoline	23
Middle distillates	25
Fuel oil	45
Other products[a]	7

[a]Includes refinery fuels and losses.

Source: British Petroleum Company, Ltd., "BP Statistical Review of the World Oil Industry 1975," 1976.

World scale or reference rates are specified for each major trade route in the world and in general vary slightly depending upon the ports utilized. However, since this analysis is concerned with the average rates experienced between major regions of the world, it is sufficient to express the 1975 world scale rates in terms of a linear regression equation as follows:

$$\text{World scale rate} = 1.26(\text{distance}) + 0.88$$

where distance is expressed in thousands of nautical miles and the rate is given in dollars per long ton.

The world scale spot market rate between the Persian Gulf and Northern Europe for crude carriers is presented in Figure 5-1 for 1974 and 1975 based on weighted average monthly figures.

The AFRA rates which are applied to these world scale values in the world energy model are as follows:

Product tankers	135
Small tankers	122
Medium tankers	81
Large tankers	63
VLCC	56

When the AFRA rates are applied to the world scale values, the results approximate the charges that were experienced in 1975. A basic assumption in the model is that the 1975 relatively depressed tanker rates will continue into the foreseeable future. This is obviously a somewhat optimistic estimate of transportation costs, and these costs could be higher by sometime in the 1980s if the demand for tankers increases substantially.

The shipping rates imposed in the world energy model are adjusted dynamically as a function of the price of bunker fuel. As the price of bunker fuel changes, the transportation costs on each route are adjusted, based upon the usage of bunker fuel on the route for each type of ship. This is accomplished by subtracting the contribution of bunker fuel to transportation costs using current fuel prices and then letting the model determine the volume of bunker fuel to be used based upon the actual usage of ships. The model consumes the appropriate quantities of bunker fuel at the prevailing price in each region. As examples, the following adjustments to tanker rates per barrel are made on the Persian Gulf-to-Rotterdam and the Persian Gulf-to-Japan routes for each $1.00 increase in the price of bunker fuel:

	Persian Gulf to Rotterdam	Persian Gulf to Japan
Small tankers	$0.046	$0.048
Medium tankers	0.062	0.047
Large tankers	0.034	0.026
VLCC	0.038	0.023

The adjustments are a function of routing as well as the efficiency of the ships. This can be seen in that the adjustment for VLCCs exceeds that for large tankers on the Persian Gulf-to-Rotterdam route because the large tankers can use the Suez Canal while in ballast whereas the VLCCs cannot.

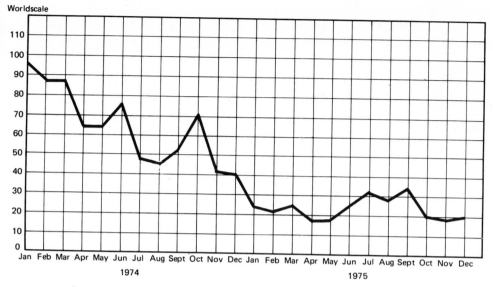

Source: John I. Jacobs & Co., Ltd., *World Tanker Fleet Review,* London, 31
December 1975.

Figure 5-1. World Scale Spot Market Rates.

The transportation costs associated with international shipments of coal
and liquefied natural gas (LNG) were estimated using Bureau of Mines data
in the case of coal and FEA data for LNG. The freight rates applied in the
model are derived using the following equations:

$$\text{Coal rate} = 1.86(\text{Distance}) + 4.96$$
$$\text{LNG rate} = 0.177(\text{Distance}) + 0.189$$

where the coal rate is expressed in dollars per long ton and the LNG rate is
expressed in dollars per thousand cubic feet of natural gas.

A summary of existing tanker fleets and those on order by size groups
and types of ownership at the end of 1975 is presented in Table 5-9. OPEC
country tanker fleets in existence and on order at the end of 1975 are
presented in Table 5-10.

Supply Parameters

The primary resources considered in the supply models are coal (various
types), crude oil (various types), and natural gas. The supply of each of

Table 5-9
World Tanker Fleet at the End of 1975: Existing and on Order, by Size

Size Group	Existing		On Order	
dwt	Number	1000 dwt	Number	1000 dwt
Under 16,999	321	4375	45	490
17,000-49,999	1639	47,472	167	5193
50,000-99,999	730	52,120	103	8016
100,000-149,999	241	29,617	69	8575
150,000-199,999	47	8127	48	7592
200,000-399,999	582	144,659	154	43,896
Over 400,000	5	2296	34	14,774
Total	3565	288,669	610	88,536

Source: John I. Jacobs Co. Ltd. "World Tanker Fleet Review," 1975.

Table 5-10
OPEC Tanker Fleet at End of 1975: Existing and on Order
(in 1000 dwt)

	200,000 dwt +				All Sizes			
	Existing		On Order		Existing		On Order	
Country	No.	dwt	No.	dwt	No.	dwt	No.	dwt
Abu Dhabi	2	531	—	—	2	531	—	—
Iraq	—	—	1	312	9	374	9	1488
Kuwait	4	984	4	1265	8	1292	4	1265
Saudi Arabia	1	269	1	274	8	728	1	274
Arab owned (other)	—	—	2	616	—	—	3	751
Iran	2	455	—	—	8	696	1	20
Egypt	—	—	—	—	8	193	—	—
Libya	—	—	1	312	5	406	8	1062
Algeria	—	—	1	380	5	274	1	380
Venezuela	—	—	—	—	14	436	1	30
Total	9	2239	10	3159	67	4930	28	5270

Source: John I. Jacobs Co. Ltd., "World Tanker Fleet Review," 1975.

these primary forms of energy for the United States is represented in the model at different minimum acceptable price increments. This price includes an average acceptable rate of return on investment, as well as transportation costs within the region from the point of production (or landing) to the center points of consumption regions. The United States supply data are those used in the PIES reference case, and were generated by the supply models presented in the preceding chapter. Because of the large volume of United States supply data, they are not presented in this chapter. Readers are referred to FEA's PIES documentation for this information.

Formal supply models, such as those for the United States, were not used for the other OECD countries because of inadequate data. A short-cut approach was used instead, as indicated in the preceding chapter. The supply forecasts for coal, oil, and gas are those reported for OECD in *Energy Prospects to 1985* for the years 1980 and 1985, assuming first that the price of OPEC oil landed in New York is $12 per barrel and then that it is $16. These prices were adjusted to a landed European price, and the quantities forecasted were also adjusted. These forecasts are in Table 5-11 for each price.

In order to generate OECD (excluding United States) supply curves for primary energy resources (represented by step functions in the model), an isoelastic function was fitted to the supply estimates at $12 and $16 (as adjusted) by considering the Btu equivalent prices for each resource assuming an initial imported oil price of $12 (as adjusted). The supply data are generated for a reference case scenario as was done for the United States.

The elasticities of supply, derived from Table 5-11, are as follows:

	1980	*1985*
Oil	0.16	0.14
Gas	0.20	0.20
Coal	0.0	0.0

The availability of OECD (excluding United States) nuclear and hydroelectric power was assumed not to be price-sensitive, and the quantities for these energy forms (see Table 5-12) serve to bound these supplies in the electricity sector of the world energy model. These elasticities more or less represent the point of view of the authors of *Energy Prospects to 1985*.

The supply estimates for oil in the noncommunist developing countries (excluding OPEC) are represented in the model by constant elasticity supply curves, as were those decribed above for OECD. The supply

Table 5-11
Selected OECD Country Indigenous Primary Energy Production,
1980 and 1985
(MMbbl/D oil equivalent)

	1980						
	$12/bbl				*$16/bbl*		
Regions	*Oil*	*Coal*	*Gas*	*Elec.*	*Oil*	*Coal*	*Gas*
Europe	2.72	3.46	3.57	1.83	2.9	3.4	3.8
Canada	1.60	0.40	1.41	0.62	1.6	0.4	1.4
Japan	0.40	0.18	0.06	0.77	0.1	0.2	0.1
	1985						
	$12/bbl				*$16/bbl*		
Regions	*Oil*	*Coal*	*Gas*	*Elec.*	*Oil*	*Coal*	*Gas*
Europe	3.46	3.81	3.57	3.98	3.6	3.8	3.8
Canada	1.34	0.60	1.38	1.18	1.4	0.6	1.4
Japan	0.06	0.20	0.06	1.82	0.1	0.2	0.1

Source: *Energy Prospects to 1985*, Paris: OECD, December 1974, as modified by the author.

Table 5-12
Electrical Generation Limits for Nuclear/Hydroelectric
(MMbbl/D of Oil Equivalent)

	1980		1985	
	$12/bbl	*$16/bbl*	*$12/bbl*	*$16/bbl*
Europe	1.8	1.9	4.0	4.0
Canada	0.6	0.7	1.2	1.2
Japan	0.8	0.8	1.8	1.9
Total	3.2	3.4	7.0	7.1

Source: *Energy Prospects to 1985,* Paris: OECD, December 1974.

elasticities were computed on the same basis as those for OECD using the quantities produced at $12 and $16. The supplies at these prices are in Table 5-13.

Net exports of oil from the communist countries are specified as point estimates and assumed not to be price-sensitive. The net export estimates, in Mbbl/D, are shown in the following tabulation.

	1980	1985
Russia	300	0
China	1000	1200

The supply of coal and gas in the non-OECD regions is assumed to grow at the same rate specified for oil consumption in those regions, or about 4.7 percent per year. The elasticity of supply for coal and gas is assumed to be 0.1 in these regions, and price is determined on a Btu equivalent basis with oil.

The supply estimates of OPEC oil as well as its price are a function of OPEC absorptive capacity for oil revenues as well as other factors. The entire subject of OPEC supply is discussed under OPEC price and production strategies in Chapter 6.

Table 5-13
Crude Oil Production in Non-OPEC Developing Countries Excluding Soviet Bloc
(MMbbl/D)

	1980		1985	
	$12/bbl	*$16/bbl*	*$12/bbl*	*$16/bbl*
Latin America	3.7	4.0	4.2	4.4
Africa	1.0	1.2	1.8	2.0
Asia	1.6	1.8	2.3	2.5
Total	6.4	7.0	8.3	8.9

Source: Federal Energy Administration, Office of International Energy Affairs, and other sources.

Results: World Demand for OPEC Oil

The major result obtained from the world energy model (oil importing countries) is the estimate of the oil-importing countries' demand for OPEC oil at different price levels set by OPEC for their oil. This demand schedule is the main input to the world energy model (OPEC member countries) for determining OPEC's price and production strategies as well as the relative stability of OPEC in the future. The demand schedule for OPEC oil is generated by a series of equilibrium analyses of importing countries' supply and demand for energy. These analyses cover a range of prices set by OPEC for its oil, given the degree of response of oil-importing countries in accelerating their production of alternative energy resources and in making other adjustments.

Two scenarios were explicitly considered in preparing this study: a business-as-usual (BAU or reference case) scenario, and an accelerated development/accelerated conservation (AD/AC) scenario. Only results for the first are discussed in this book. The BAU scenario (or reference case) is examined for OPEC prices ranging from $7 to $15 (in 1975 U.S. dollars f.o.b. Persian Gulf). The scenario assumes continuation of the status quo and, in particular, that no special extra efforts are made by producers, consumers, and governments of the oil-importing countries to accelerate development of alternative energy resources or to adopt conservation measures in response to changes in the price of OPEC oil.

At each price for imported oil, supply and demand for the energy-consuming regions interact in order to determine how much oil imports from OPEC member countries are necessary to bring supply and demand into equilibrium for each geographic region. The supply and demand for alternative energy forms in the various geographic regions are determined by their respective price and income elasticities. Given the price-sensitive supply schedule for each primary form of energy and for each geographic region, and given the price elasticities of demand for energy and those demand forecasts unrestricted by such elasticities, the equilibrium price, demand, and supply for each form of energy in each region are determined.

Of course, an unlimited number of cases or scenarios could be examined by changing the various parameters of supply, demand, distribution, and conversion technologies. However, in this book, the analysis is limited to the BAU scenario.

A vast amount of detailed output was generated by the model for equilibrium demand, supply, and prices for all energy forms for each geographic region for 1980 and 1985. For illustration, the 1980 and 1985 equilibrium supply, demand, and imports for $11 imported oil (f.o.b. Persian Gulf) for the BAU case is presented in Table 5-14. The data are

Table 5-14
World Energy Balance and Demand for OPEC Oil: 1980 and 1985
(MMbbl/D of oil equivalent)

		1980					1985				
		Coal	Oil	Natural Gas	Hydro/ nuclear	Total	Coal	Oil	Natural Gas	Hydro/ nuclear	Total
U.S.	Consumption	8.5	20.1	9.6	3.9	42.1	10.2	21.9	10.1	6.4	48.6
	Production	8.8	10.9	9.3	3.9	32.9	10.9	12.1	8.9	6.4	38.3
	Net Imports	-0.3	9.2	0.3	—	9.2	-0.7	9.8	1.2	—	10.3
Other OECD	Consumption	8.3	27.1	6.8	6.3	48.5	9.1	31.9	8.4	9.7	59.1
	Production	6.3	6.2	5.3	6.3	23.9	7.3	6.5	6.2	9.7	29.7
	Net Imports	2.0	20.9	1.5	—	24.6	1.8	25.4	2.2	—	29.4
Rest of World, Excluding OPEC and Communist Countries	Consumption	2.8	8.2	1.6	0.6	13.2	3.1	10.6	2.0	0.8	16.5
	Production	2.6	6.1	1.8	0.6	11.1	2.9	9.1	2.2	0.8	15.0
	Net Imports	-0.2	2.1	-0.2	—	2.1	0.2	1.5	-0.2	—	1.5
OPEC	Consumption	0.1	2.6	0.4	0.1	3.2	0.2	4.0	0.7	0.1	5.0
	Production	0.1	35.3	2.4	0.1	37.9	0.2	40.7	3.5	0.1	44.5
	Net Exports	—	32.7	2.0	—	34.7	—	36.7	2.8	—	39.5

Note: (1) Excludes bunker fuel and stock changes.
(2) Based on business-as-usual case with $11 OPEC oil (f.o.b. Persian Gulf) in constant 1975 U.S. Dollars.

reported for the United States, other OECD countries, the rest of the world excluding OPEC and the communist countries, and finally OPEC member countries; and for coal, oil, natural gas, hydro/nuclear, and the total. The oil-importing countries' demand schedule for OPEC oil at alternative price levels for the BAU scenario is presented in Table 5-15.

Table 5-15
Demand for OPEC Oil by Oil-Importing Countries (Reference Case)

Crude Price, U.S. $/bbl		Demand, MMbbl/D	
f.o.b. Persian Gulf	U.S. C.I.F. Price[a]	1980	1985
$7.00	$9.00	39.2	42.4
9.00	11.00	36.3	40.2
11.00	13.00	32.7	36.7
13.00	15.00	30.5	35.1
15.00	17.00	29.1	32.3

[a]Transportation cost between Persian Gulf and United States East Coast is assumed to be $2.00 per barrel.
Note: Prices in constant 1975 U.S. Dollars.

**Part III
World Energy Model: OPEC Member
Countries**

6

OPEC Price and Production Strategies

The world energy model presented in Part II dealt with the supply and demand for alternative forms of energy in the oil-importing regions. The future energy import requirements of the oil-importing countries (mainly imported oil) for each region were estimated at different assumed or expected levels of OPEC prices. Those price-quantity relationships constitute the demand curve for OPEC oil.[1] The oil-importing countries expect that their entire demand will be satisfied by OPEC member countries. This expectation is realistic only if the OPEC member countries have an unlimited need for oil revenues. In reality, there are substantial differences in the ability of OPEC countries to absorb oil revenues, as well as differences in goals. Thus, the oil-importing countries will interface with an organization that has a cartel structure rather than a monopoly structure.

The purpose of the world energy model (OPEC member countries) developed in this part of the book is to determine the price and production strategies of individual OPEC member countries. It determines whether OPEC members with diverse strategies would collectively produce crude oil above, below, or at the levels demanded from them by the oil-importing countries.

Analysis of OPEC's market structure, price, and production strategies has important implications for domestic energy policies and programs of oil-importing countries. Researchers and policy makers are aware of the significance of this subject, and several studies have already been published in this area including Blitzer, Meeraus, and Stoutjesdijk;[2] Ezzati;[3] Cremer and Weitzman;[4] Kalymon;[5] and Kennedy.[6] Some of these studies treat OPEC as a cohesive monopoly and forecast a revenue-maximizing price and production strategy for OPEC. Others analyze OPEC's price and production strategies in a static environment, for a particular year in the future. Almost all these studies have highly simplified representations of energy markets in the oil-importing countries. Such analyses are inadequate and grossly misrepresent the peculiar characteristics of OPEC. Given the difference in economic infrastructure, in oil reserves, in population, and in the need for oil revenues among OPEC countries, OPEC can hardly be categorized as a monopoly. A cartel approach to the analysis of future OPEC price and production strategies is more realistic than is a monopoly approach. The apparent reason why a monopoly approach has usually been selected in previous studies is that monopoly markets have been covered extensively in the economic literature. Similarly, the selection of static rather than dynamic analysis in these studies is due to the simplicity of the former approach.

For many OPEC member countries, oil revenues for domestic investment are preferable to foreign investment. They believe that oil revenues in excess of domestic development needs will be exposed to devaluation, inflation, expropriation, and give-away in terms of free loans or grants; that they will induce excessive military expenditures and downward pressure on world crude oil prices; and that future generations will be denied adequate oil resources. The highly limited absorptive capacity of some member countries is as important as the virtually unlimited absorptive capacity of others in determining future OPEC price and production strategies. Countries with limited absorptive capacity can exert an upward pressure on crude oil prices by cutting back production, and those with higher absorptive capacity can exert downward pressure on prices by increasing their crude oil production to satisfy their oil revenue needs. Thus, OPEC price and production policies will be heavily influenced by the ability of individual OPEC countries to absorb oil revenues.

This chapter adopts a more plausible approach and analyzes OPEC's price and production strategies within a dynamic, special cartel theory based on the ability of individual member countries to absorb oil revenues for the purpose of importing, consuming, and investing and also based on their economic infrastructure, volumes of oil reserves, and potential production.[7] The model generates a crude oil production prorationing program for the OPEC member countries based on their absorptive capacity, economic infrastructure, population, size of oil revenues, and present and potential production capacities only in the event that the sum of crude oil production of OPEC member countries is expected to become greater than the amount demanded from them by the oil-importing countries. Further, the model is constructed in a way that allows for a joint OPEC fund from which side payments (in terms of very low-interest-rate loans) could be made to members in order to discourage them from producing more than their ration and in order to prevent OPEC as a whole from producing more than what is demanded from it.

The following section presents a theoretical analysis of OPEC price and production strategies under different market structures followed by the OPEC oil supply model.

Analysis of OPEC Price and Production Strategies under Alternative Market Structures

The highly refined state of monopoly theory in the economic literature has induced many writers on OPEC price and production strategies to treat OPEC as a monopoly.[8] They have used the market equilibrium conditions for a monopoly as criteria for determining OPEC's future price and production strategies. This condition is briefly explained in the following section.

OPEC as a Monopoly

Under monopoly conditions, it is assumed that OPEC member countries have unified goals, that they collectively set prices for crude oil, that there is no substantial price competition among them, and that differences in the quality of their crudes are reflected in prices. The "competitive fringe" are non-OPEC suppliers, including the United States, Canada, USSR, Mexico,[9] etc., which are price takers. Either the members of the "competitive fringe" are also crude oil importers, or else their exports are too small to individually influence world crude oil prices set by OPEC. The members of the competitive fringe will increase their output to a level where their short-term marginal cost equalizes the price of crude oil set by OPEC, adjusted for crude oil quality differentials and transportation costs. OPEC sets crude oil prices by taking into account non-OPEC crude oil supplies and costs. OPEC equilibrium price and production under monopoly are presented in Figure 6-1.

The demand for OPEC oil by the oil-importing countries (excess demand, ED) has been obtained as a difference between the world demand and non-OPEC supply of energy at different levels of OPEC prices. The marginal revenue (MR) curve for OPEC oil is derived from the effective demand (ED) curve for such oil. Marginal cost of oil production by OPEC is represented by MC.

In the short-run, OPEC's profit will be maximized if members collectively produce Q_1 at price P_1, where OPEC marginal cost equals marginal revenue. At price P_1, OPEC will produce $0Q_1$. At price P_2, non-OPEC energy supplies will satisfy non-OPEC needs.

The preceding analysis indicates that in the short run OPEC will adjust its

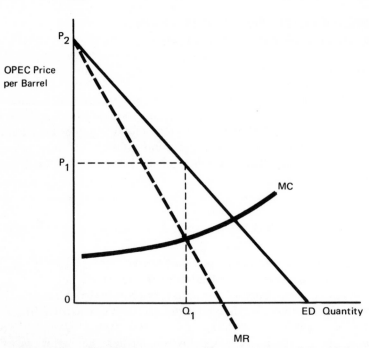

Figure 6-1. OPEC Short-Term Revenue-Maximizing Price Strategy as a Monopolist.

price until marginal revenue equals marginal cost. But if this price is high enough to generate positive economic profits for the competitive fringe, then in the long run new oil fields will be discovered and new alternative energy forms will be developed. Further, the demand for petroleum products is more price-elastic in the long run than in the short run as a result of competition from newly developed or expanded alternative energy forms such as oil shale and coal, consumer reaction toward higher prices, and all other factors related to adjustment lags on both demand and supply sides of the market such as changes in stock of fuel-consuming equipment and development of new technology. As a result, the optimum long-run OPEC price and output strategy will be different from $MR = MC$. Under certain conditions, which will be discussed in the following section, OPEC may discourage new competition while retaining supernormal profits. The main question for OPEC under these conditions is how far above costs price can be maintained without inducing development of alternative energy forms.

Stated simply, the monopoly theory approach states that OPEC will select price and production strategies in such a way as to maximize its net revenue. OPEC will supply all the crude oil demanded from it by oil-importing countries at a net revenue-maximizing price set by OPEC. In other words, given the net revenue-maximizing price, demand for OPEC oil determined as the difference between world demand and non-OPEC supply for crude oil.[10] Once OPEC sets crude oil prices its production of crude oil is determined by the price elasticities of world demand and non-OPEC supply of crude oil. This analysis is shown in Figures 6-2 and 6-3. Figure 6-2 depicts world demand and non-OPEC supply curves for crude oil at different price levels for OPEC oil. The horizontal distance between the two curves represents the demand for OPEC oil, which is also depicted in Figure 6-3. As a monopolist, OPEC will produce at the point on the demand curve which maximizes its net revenue.

OPEC is also frequently viewed as a residual or swing producer. In this (nonmonopoly) situation, its supply curve will be coincident with the demand curve for OPEC oil.

OPEC as a Revenue Maximizer through Limit Pricing

The previous discussion that OPEC as a monopoly will adjust its output until marginal revenue equals marginal costs holds true in the short run. If the price set by OPEC is high enough to generate positive economic profits for the competitive fringe, then in the long run new oil fields will be discovered and alternative energy forms will be developed.

Under conditions discussed below, OPEC may discourage new competition while retaining supernormal profits. Under this circumstance, OPEC's optimal pricing and output policy is determined. In Figure 6-4, the *DD* curve represents the demand for OPEC oil (total world demand minus the supply from the competitive fringe).

OPEC Pricing above the Entry Deterrent Level. Let us assume that OPEC will act as a dominant price-setting cartel, that the competitive fringe members are price takers, and that the output from individual fringe countries does not have any significant influence on world crude oil prices. Further, assume that the minimum average total cost per unit, including normal profit, for the competitive fringe is $0P_c$, (i.e., for the moment assume that the long-run competitive supply function is perfectly elastic) and that all potential fringe producers achieve this cost level. Any prices set by OPEC above P_c will generate supernormal profits for the competitive fringe and attract new entrants such that OPEC's demand curve will shift to the left and eventually to $P_c FD'$ (the long term demand curve for OPEC) if

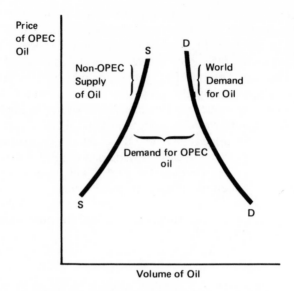

Figure 6-2. World Demand and Non-OPEC
Supply of Oil.

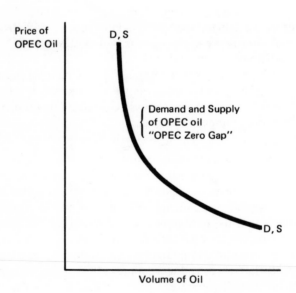

Figure 6-3. Demand and Supply for OPEC Oil
under Monopoly and When OPEC Is a
Residual Producer.

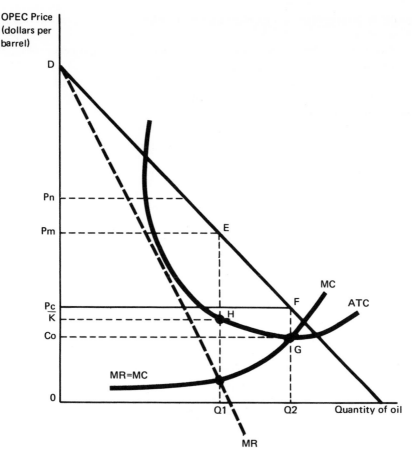

Figure 6-4. OPEC Revenue Maximization through Limit Pricing.

OPEC keeps prices above P_c long enough. $0P_c$, the lowest attainable total unit cost for the competitive fringe, is the entry deterrent or limit price level.[11]

OPEC Pricing at the Entry Deterrent Level. As a second alternative, OPEC can select price and output strategies that will prevent the above extreme situation. OPEC can keep the competitive fringe in check by setting crude oil prices slightly below P_c. The long-run profit expectations of OPEC depend upon how long they can keep their production costs well below the P_c competitive fringe unit costs. The present very low cost of production indicates that OPEC can set prices at or slightly below P_c and earn supernormal profits while deterring the development of alternative energy resources.

Assume that OPEC operates on a combined short-run average total cost function *ATC,* with corresponding marginal cost *MC,* and produces Q_2 compatible with price P_c. The unit cost of OPEC at Q_2 is C_0. OPEC can earn total profits of P_cFGC_0 per period while preventing new development of alternative energy resources.

In choosing a price policy, therefore, OPEC must compare the initially lower but persistent profits from an entry-limiting strategy against the initially higher but eventually lower profits from the short-run maximization strategy. The decision depends upon both the size of P_cFGC_0 as opposed to P_mEHK and the discount rate applied to future earnings. In the OPEC case, discount rates play a decisive role. High discount rates place little weight on future profits and are appropriate when the future is uncertain, such as when planning a long-range pricing policy.

OPEC as a Cartel

The above approaches to determining OPEC's price and production strategies assume that OPEC is a completely cohesive unit and that there will be uniformity and unanimity among members in their future price and production policy decisions. This is a very unrealistic assumption, and application of monopoly theory to OPEC price and production strategies does not represent the actual interaction between OPEC members, and ignores the substantial economic, social, and political differences among them. A cartel theory in which both the similarities and the differences among OPEC members are reflected in their future price and production strategies is more applicable in this circumstance.

OPEC's future stability is dependent upon how closely the OPEC cartel can be made to approximate a monopoly by eliminating certain differences between members and unifying their goals. One means of achieving this is through an effective and widely accepted production prorationing program. An alternative is to establish a joint OPEC fund from which side payments (in terms of very low-interest-rate loans) would be made to members in order to discourage them from producing more than their ration and in order to prevent OPEC as a whole from producing more than what is demanded from it. Other developments, such as greater political unity or the establishment of regional economic pacts, would minimize the conflict among member countries and bring the OPEC cartel closer to an OPEC monopoly.

Unfortunately, the theory of cartels is not well developed in the economic literature mainly because many varieties of cartels could be developed and no unified theory could likely cover all of them.[12]

This study attempts to assess OPEC's stability and its future price and production strategies by considering member country differences in economic infrastructure; in capacity to absorb oil revenues into their economies in the form of imports, investment, and consumption; and in the volume of crude oil reserves and production potential. At any given price, the model determines how much crude oil production is required by each OPEC member country to satisfy its economic needs. It then determines whether the sum of the exports of the members collectively is less than or greater than what has been demanded from them by the oil-importing countries. The excess production (if any) over demand for OPEC oil, at any given price, is called the *destruction gap*. This gap, if it continues to exist for a time, will lead to a downward pressure on OPEC crude oil prices and a weakness in or even a disintegration of OPEC. This would reflect the fact that differences among OPEC members had led the cartel to the opposite end of the spectrum—cartel disintegration or competitive market—rather than toward monopoly or a more stable cartel. The model developed in this book devises production prorationing and side-payment schemes to counteract disintegrative tendencies. They are based on the economic infrastructure of the members ot the cartel, their ability to absorb oil revenues into their economies, and the size of crude oil reserves and production potential. The production prorationing scheme, if accepted, would bring the OPEC cartel toward a monopoly situation with *zero gap* where supply and demand for OPEC oil are identical. Figure 6-5 depicts this situation. After the prorationing program is implemented, Figure 6-5 would be similar to Figure 6-3 of the monopoly case.

On the other hand, the sum of the crude oil production generated by the model for any given level of price for each member country may be less than the total volume of oil demanded from OPEC as a whole by the oil-importing countries. This deficit in production over demand is called a *stability gap*. The size of this gap, if maintained for some time, may lead to an upward pressure on OPEC crude oil prices and to greater strength and stability for the OPEC cartel. Figure 6-6 depicts this situation.

When demand and supply for OPEC oil intersect, the destruction or stability gap may be below or above the point of intersection, depending upon the elasticity of demand and supply of OPEC oil. Figures 6-7 and 6-8 depict these situations. Figure 6-7 implies that the supply elasticity is smaller than the demand elasticity for OPEC oil. In this situation, the stability gap is below and the destruction gap is above the point of intersection. If initially OPEC operates within the stability gap, a subsequent reduction in production and increase in prices may lead OPEC to the destruction gap or to a weakening of OPEC. If OPEC is in the destruction gap, the only way it can be stabilized is by reducing prices and increasing production. In Figure 6-8, the supply elasticity is greater than the demand elasticity for OPEC oil. In this circumstance, the destruction gap is below

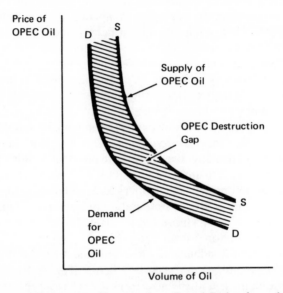

Figure 6-5. Destructive Cartel Behavior which Requires Prorationing for Stability.

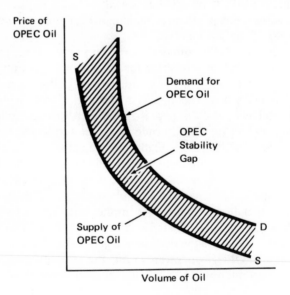

Figure 6-6. Cartel Behavior which Leads to Further Strengthening.

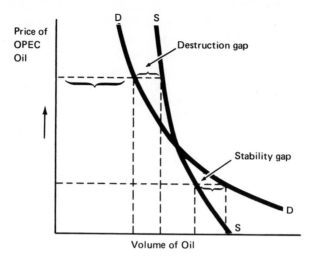

Figure 6-7. Higher Prices Move OPEC out of Stability Gap into Destruction Gap and Weaken OPEC Position.

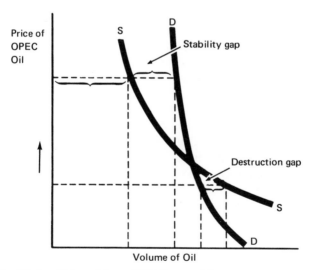

Figure 6-8. Higher Prices Move OPEC out of Destruction Gap into Stability Gap and Strengthen OPEC Position.

and the stability gap is above the point of intersection. This circumstance is very unusual. That is, if OPEC is in the destruction gap, further price increases and production cutbacks could bring OPEC out of the destruction gap to stability; and if OPEC is in the stability gap, further price increases and production cutbacks could lead to further strengthening of OPEC.

The model developed in this book determines crude oil production requirements by individual OPEC member countries at different price levels, given that their goal is to maximize the present value of their future welfare. Such determination is made subject to each country's economic parameters. The associated values generated for the growth in GDP, imports, and other economic indicators should be evaluated only in the context of the present framework rather than being treated as unconditional forecasts. The model then calculates the sum of individual member countries' crude oil production and devises a production prorationing scheme when necessary.

Another distinct advantage of the model developed in this chapter over the monopoly approach to OPEC's price and production is that it is time-dynamic. Most previous analyses of future OPEC price and production policies are static and do not trace OPEC's behavior through time.

OPEC Oil Supply Model

This section presents the structure of the OPEC oil price and production strategy model. It is a dynamic (intertemporal), multisectoral, empirical linear programming model. The objective function of the model is to maximize the joint weighted social welfare function of OPEC member countries over time. The constraints of the model represent a novel approach. They consist of macroeconometric models of each OPEC member country linked to the demand for OPEC oil (world excess demand for oil) non-OPEC supplies and prices, and OPEC revenues and production of crude oil. Although the macroeconometric models are estimated as equalities, they are then expressed as inequalities for use as constraints of the linear programming model, of which they are a part. The inequalities state that the proportional relationship between the left-hand and right-hand sides of equations in the historical period will be maintained or exceeded in future periods. Conceptually, this potential change is effected by changing the constant terms to ensure a solution for the entire model.

The use of inequalities in the macroeconometric models is useful for developing countries, especially those that have access to large amounts of foreign exchange relative to what was available in recent historical periods. The use of historically estimated equality relationships would unduly restrict their expected future rapid economic growth.

The linear programming model simultaneously solves for all OPEC member country crude oil production requirements given that the objective function is to maximize the present value of future welfare. Solution values for associated economic indicators, such as GNP and imports, are also determined.

The model allows sensitivity analysis of parameters of the model, such as price and income elasticities of world demand, non-OPEC supply of crude oil, OPEC prices and demand for OPEC oil, capital-output ratios, rates of return on foreign assets, discount rates of future consumption, consumption weights for each country (based on socioeconomic characteristics), and other policy variables.

Briefly, the model works as follows. First, at any given OPEC crude oil price level, world demand and non-OPEC supply of primary energy and energy products are simulated based on given price and income elasticities. Second, the demand (excess demand) for OPEC oil is derived by subtracting non-OPEC energy supply from world energy demand at the OPEC price. Third, the model determines crude oil production for each member country based on its revenue needs and economic infrastructure. Fourth, the sum of each individual OPEC country's production is compared to the demand for OPEC oil. If the production is in excess of what has been demanded, either the production level equivalent to the demand will be prorationed among the member countries based on their absorptive capacity for oil revenue and economic infrastructure, or a side-payment plan will be placed into effect. If the production is less than what has been demanded, there will be pressure for OPEC to increase its price.

The relationships and constraints of the linear programming model are grouped into the following major categories.

1. The objective function
2. Petroleum equations
3. Behavioral macroeconometric relationships
4. Definitional equations
5. Policy equations

Each group of equations is discussed below. The variables and input parameters are presented in Tables 6-1 and 6-2.

Joint Objective Function

The objective function of the model is to maximize the weighted sum of the utility functions of OPEC member countries. Each country's utility function is based on the present value of future consumption over the

Table 6-1
Variables and Subscripts in the OPEC Oil Supply Model

Linear Programming and Econometric Variables

CG	=	Government consumption
CP	=	Private consumption
CS	=	Capital stock
CT	=	Total consumption
DO	=	Quantity of domestic crude oil consumption
DP	=	Depreciation
ED	=	World demand for OPEC oil (excess demand)
FN	=	Net factor payments
FT	=	Factor payments to abroad
GD	=	Gross domestic product
GN	=	Gross national product
IG	=	Government investment
IP	=	Private investment
IT	=	Total investment
MT	=	Total imports of goods and services
NS	=	Non-OPEC supply of energy
OU	=	Domestic output
PR	=	OPEC price of crude oil
QT	=	Quantity of oil produced
RS	=	Proved oil reserves
TD	=	Direct taxes
TI	=	Indirect taxes
TP	=	Total government take from oil
TT	=	Total tax receipts by government
VN	=	Nonpetroleum gross domestic value added
VP	=	Value of petroleum produced
VX	=	Value of petroleum exports
W	=	Value of the objective function for OPEC
WD	=	World demand for energy
wt	=	Weight of the objective function for an OPEC member
XC	=	Foreign investment (net flow)
XN	=	Value of nonpetroleum exports

Table 6-1 (Continued)

XP	=	Quantity of petroleum exports
YD	=	Disposable income

Subscripts		
n	=	1, 2, . . . , N OPEC member countries
t	=	1, 2, . . . , T time periods of planning horizon
p	=	1, 2, . . . , ∞ time periods of postplanning horizon

Table 6-2
Input Parameters of OPEC Oil Supply Model

$(GN)_{t-1}$ $(CG)_{t-1}$ $(CT)_{t-1}$ $(IT)_{t-1}$ (a_j, b_j, γ_j)	=	Represent the coefficients for a particular country, where j is the index for an equation in each country
r	=	Interest rate on foreign assets
i	=	Discount rate for consumption
β	=	Weight for terminal-year income incorporating discount procedure for future consumption
m	=	Maximum feasible rate of growth in capital (policy variable)
p	=	Rate of population growth (policy variable)
h	=	Maximum percentage of oil revenue planned to be invested outside the country (policy variable)
MC	=	Marginal cost of crude oil
OT	=	OPEC take per barrel
wt	=	Consumption weight for each country
DE	=	Price elasticity of demand
IE	=	Income elasticity of demand
SE	=	Price elasticity of supply
DG	=	Rate of growth in demand
SG	=	Rate of growth in supply
OK	=	Output capital ratio
WD_0	=	Initial world demand for oil
PR_0	=	Initial price of oil
NS_0	=	Initial non-OPEC supply of oil
XC_0	=	Initial capital stock in foreign investment

planning horizon. The weight assigned to each country's consumption depends upon many factors, including the size of oil reserves, population, etc. This weight can be changed parametrically to measure its impact on OPEC's policy decisions and other variables in the model. The other component of the objective function is the feasible sustainable rate of growth in GNP in the postplanning period.

Different welfare assumptions are represented by the values assigned to the parameters in the objective function. For example, if an OPEC member country has a high preference for improvement of living standards during the planning period compared to concern for living standards in the distant future, a relatively low weight would be assigned to postplan terminal-year consumption. The discount rates used in the objective function are based upon the standard time preference argument, i.e., a higher discount rate in later years which is consistent with diminishing marginal utility of consumption. The joint objective function is as follows:[13]

$$\text{Maximize} \quad W = \sum_{n=1}^{N} \sum_{t=1}^{T} |(wt)_{n,t} \frac{(CT)_{n,t}}{(1+i)_{n,t}^{t}} + \beta(GN)_{n,T} \qquad (6.1)$$

where

$$\beta = \delta (1 - \alpha) \sum_{p=1}^{\infty} \frac{(1 + \zeta)^p}{(1 + d)^{T+p}}$$

δ = weight on postplan consumption
α = marginal saving rate
d = rate of discount of postplan consumption
β = weight for terminal-year income incorporating discount procedure for postplanning period consumption
ζ = postplan growth rate in GNP

In this study, the value derived for the objective function (W) is not used explicitly in the analysis. However, the objective function as a whole will influence the paths of the variables in the model. The expression $\beta(GN)_{n,T}$ is the terminal condition. It ensures availability of resources for the postplanning period.[14] The following paragraphs describe each of the relationships of the model and their role in the entire model.

Petroleum Equations

The excess demand curve for OPEC oil plays a central role in evaluating price-output strategies of OPEC and its stability, as well as the many other issues involving international energy markets. The excess demand for OPEC oil (or simply the demand for oil facing OPEC, or export of OPEC oil at a price) is defined as the difference between the world demand (*WD*) and the non-OPEC supply of energy (*NS*) at a given price for OPEC oil. The excess demand curve (*ED*) is constructed by plotting quantities of excess demand at various price levels.

$$(ED)_t = (WD)_t - (NS)_t \tag{6.2}$$

The excess-demand curve used in the OPEC supply oil model (world energy model—OPEC member countries) is generated from the world energy model (oil-importing countries) presented in Part III. There is no need to emphasize the importance of generating the excess-demand curve for OPEC oil with a comprehensive regionally and sectorally disaggregated world energy model. It allows for representation of differences in regional price and income elasticities and growth rates of supply and demand for various energy forms. It explicitly incorporates the technology of fuel substitution and conversion as well as its supply and transportation. It introduces commercial elements, thereby approximating more closely the actual market mechanism and interactions within and between regions of the world. Thus, the pattern of energy flows associated with the demand for OPEC oil is also determined.

In order to generate an excess-demand curve, a level of OPEC take is initially assumed and the world energy model for oil-importing countries determines the equilibrium energy flows between regions by taking into account interfuel competition and interresource substitutions of alternative energy forms. The flow determines net exports or imports of energy for each region. (See Chapter 4 and 5.)

Total government revenues from petroleum for individual OPEC members are estimated as a function of the volume of petroleum exports.

$$(TP)_{n,t} = a_3 + OT(XP)_{n,t} \tag{6.3}$$

OT, the coefficient for the volume of petroleum exports, represents the OPEC take, or price, per barrel.

The value of petroleum exports is estimated as the OPEC take per barrel (*OT*) plus the marginal cost per barrel (*MC*) times the total exports of each country.

$$(VX)_{n,t} = (OT + MC) \cdot (XP)_{n,t} \qquad (6.4)$$

The total value of petroleum produced is the sum of the value of domestic petroleum consumption in each country and the value of petroleum exports.

$$(VP)_{n,t} = (PR)(DO)_{n,t} + (VX)_{n,t} \qquad (6.5)$$

Domestic oil demand for each country is expressed as a function of GNP.

$$(DO)_{n,t} \geq a_6 + b_6(GN)_{n,t} \qquad (6.6)$$

The quantity of oil produced in each country is the sum of the volumes of oil exported and consumed in the country.

$$(QT)_{n,t} = (XP)_{n,t} + (DO)_{n,t} \qquad (6.7)$$

A constraint is imposed in order to make sure that the volume of oil produced during the planning horizon does not become greater than the proved oil reserves.

$$\sum_{t=1}^{T} (QT)_{n,t} \leq (RS)_{n,t} \qquad (6.8)$$

Behavioral Macroeconometric Relationships (Constraints)

OPEC member countries' investment strategies are closely linked to their desire for diversification and the rising absorptive capacity of their economies. The investment consists of government expenditures on social overhead and investment in developmental projects. The major source of financing such expenditures is oil revenues, most of which accrue to governments rather than to the private sector. Other sources of financing are direct and indirect taxes, revenues from foreign investments, and borrowing from international and domestic institutions. Government investment is estimated as a function of its oil revenues.

$$(IG)_{n,t} \geq a_9 + b_9(TP)_{n,t} \qquad (6.9)$$

The inequality sign reflects the hypothesis that future government investment (or propensity to invest) should at least maintain the same proportional relationship with its total oil revenues as in the historical period. For similar reasons, the inequality sign has been adopted for most of the behavioral relationships of the model. The major determinants of private investment decisions in developed countries are profit expectation, rate of interest, existing stock of capital, excess capacity, level of income, technological change, marginal efficiency of capital and amount of government investment. However, in developing countries, such as OPEC countries, the role of some of these variables is not significant because of the absence of a fully developed market economy. Private sector investment in these economies is estimated as a function of preceding-period gross national product.

$$(IP)_{n,t} \geq a_{10} + b_{10}(GN)_{n,t-1} \tag{6.10}$$

Government consumption consists of purchases of goods and services to provide social, administrative, and military services. The underlying factors in government consumption are different from those for the private sector. Government expenditures depend upon government revenues from direct, indirect, and petroleum taxes; size and distribution of national income and population; and military and political factors. Certain types of consumption expenditures—notably defense, social transfer payments, and government salaries—could have little direct effect on the productivity or employment of the rest of the economy. But expenditures on items such as health and education (human and physical resources) would have the maximum impact on long-run economic growth by improving the infrastructure and the productivity of nonoil sectors. Government expenditures in OPEC countries are estimated as a function of total government revenues from all sources and the previous level of government consumption.

$$(CG)_{n,t} \geq a_{11} + b_{11}(TT)_{n,t} + \gamma_{11}(CG)_{n,t-1} \tag{6.11}$$

Private consumption expenditures are estimated as a function of personal disposable income.

$$(CP)_{n,t} \geq a_{12} + b_{12}(YD)_{n,t} \tag{6.12}$$

OPEC imports of capital goods, consumer goods, and military goods and services have increased drastically in recent years as a result of the large amount of oil revenues earned and the implementation of massive developmental projects. These goods and services have been used in some studies as a measure of the ability of OPEC countries to absorb oil revenues.[15] Absorptive capacity is recognized to be a major determinant of OPEC price and output strategies, of the future stability of OPEC, and of the availability of surplus petrodollars for foreign investment.

Imports of consumer goods for both high- and low-absorber OPEC member countries are expected to rise sharply because of the shortage of domestic consumer products, the increase in disposable family income, and the need for more variety and better-quality consumer goods.[16] However, as time passes, the rate of growth of imports of consumer goods is expected to decline as demand for more durable consumer goods declines and/or domestically produced goods enter the market. At that time, it is expected that governments may levy taxes on imported goods to protect domestically produced goods. (See Figure 6-9.)

The initial growth of capital goods imports is small for low-absorber oil-producing countries because of inadequate economic infrastructures, insufficient technical expertise, skilled labor, managerial capabilities, and other institutional problems in these countries. However, in the long run, as their infrastructure become stronger and the complementary factor inputs become available, a sharp rise in growth of capital goods imports is expected. On the other hand, the higher-absorber oil-exporting countries import substantial amounts of capital goods initially in order to support their development projects. In the longer run, it is expected that this trend will slow down. (See Figure 6-10.)

Imports of goods and services are expressed as a function of GNP. Although the importance of the composition of imports warrants an analysis of imports by various Standard International Trade Classification (SITC) groupings, such a detailed approach is deferred for future study.

$$(MT)_{n,t} \geq a_{13} + b_{13}(GN)_{n,t} \tag{6.13}$$

Exports of nonpetroleum goods in the oil-producing countries are estimated as a function of nonpetroleum gross domestic value added.

$$(XN)_{n,t} = a_{14} + b_{14}(VN)_{n,t} \tag{6.14}$$

The nonpetroleum exports of some OPEC member countries are much greater than for other members. Most of these exports are nonindustrial goods.

Factor payments to abroad consist of profits made by foreign investors which are not retained in OPEC member countries and wages earned by foreign personnel in the OPEC member countries and transferred abroad. Factor payments to abroad are expressed as a function of the value of oil produced.

$$(FT)_{n,t} = a_{15} + b_{15}(VP)_{n,t} \tag{6.15}$$

The net factor payment is the difference between factor payments from and to abroad. This includes revenues from oil invested abroad.

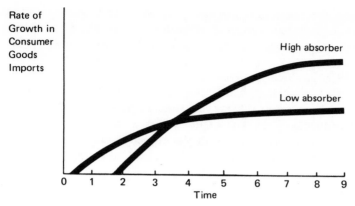

Figure 6-9. Expected General Growth Pattern in Imports of Consumer Goods by OPEC.

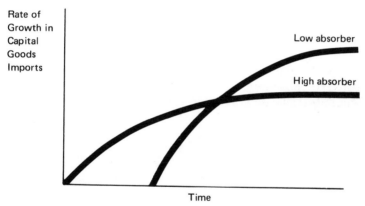

Figure 6-10. Expected General Growth Pattern in Imports of Capital Goods by OPEC.

$$(FN)_{n,t} = (FT)_{n,t} - r \left[\sum_{t=1}^{T-1} (XC)_{n,t} + (XC)_{n,0} \right] \qquad (6.16)$$

where r represents rate of return on foreign investment and XC is foreign investment (net flow).

Capital inflow and outflow may take several forms in this model. One is between OPEC member countries and the consuming countries in the form of direct and indirect investments. Such investments are constrained by the need for oil revenues within OPEC domestic economies, risks involved in foreign investments, and many other factors. The second type of capital flow is in the form of loans between the OPEC member countries themselves. Such loans are granted with very low interest rates as a side payment to discourage a country with high absorptive capacity and crude oil production potential from producing more than the share allocated to it under OPEC production prorationing.

OPEC's government revenues consist of direct, indirect, and petroleum taxes as well as returns from investments made abroad. Government revenue from direct taxes is expressed as a function of gross national product. Unlike direct taxes in developed countries, those in less developed countries are levied mostly on real estate properties.

$$(TD)_{n,t} = a_{17} + b_{17}(GN)_{n,t} \qquad (6.17)$$

Government revenues from indirect taxes consist of the fees levied on goods imported into the country. Thus, government indirect tax revenues are expressed as a function of the total value of imports.

$$(TI)_{n,t} = a_{18} + b_{18}(MT)_{n,t} \qquad (6.18)$$

OPEC government revenues from petroleum and foreign investments are presented in the definitional and petroleum equations sections.

A relatively simple production function is used in the model. It relates growth in output to capital through the output-capital ratio (OK).

$$(GD)_{n,t} - (GD)_{n,t-1} \leq (OK)_{n,t} \cdot \left[(IT)_{n,t-1} - (DP)_{n,t} \right] \qquad (6.19)$$

It is clear that more research is necessary to formulate superior production functions. The Cobb-Douglas, CES, and Translog production functions as well as input-output are among the more popular types of production functions in the economic literature. Considering the nature of the OPEC member country economies, a suitable modification of the above formulation would be to build an input-output table for the major economic sectors of the OPEC member countries. The input-output structure could easily be incorporated into the present model structure.

Definitional Equations

There are several definitional equations in the model.

Total investment in each country is the sum of private and public investment.

$$(IT)_{n,t} = (IP)_{n,t} + (IG)_{n,t} \qquad (6.20)$$

Total consumption expenditure is the sum of consumption by private and public sectors.

$$(CT)_{n,t} = (CP)_{n,t} + (CG)_{n,t} \tag{6.21}$$

The oil revenues available to most OPEC member countries are more than could be effectively absorbed by their domestic economies in the short run. For some countries, this constraint also applies to the long run. For countries like Kuwait, Qatar, and the United Arab Emirates, a well-balanced foreign portfolio of foreign financial assets may offer an attractive basis for sustained revenue to support a rising standard of living. Total government revenues is the sum of the direct, indirect, and petroleum taxes plus the revenue or interest on foreign investments.

$$(TT)_{n,t} = (TD)_{n,t} + (TI)_{n,\,t} + (TP)_{n,t} + r\left[\sum_{t=1}^{T} (XC)_{n,t} + (XC)_{n,0}\right] \tag{6.22}$$

where r represents rate of return on foreign investments.

Disposable income can be derived by subtracting total government revenues and depreciation from gross national product.

$$(YD)_{n,t} = (GN)_{n,t} - (TT)_{n,t} - (DP)_{n,t} \tag{6.23}$$

Depreciation is assumed to be a constant percentage of GNP.

$$(DP)_{n,t} = a_{24}(GN)_{n,t} \tag{6.24}$$

Value added in the nonpetroleum sector is defined as gross domestic product less the value of petroleum exports. *Gross domestic product* is defined as GNP plus net factor payments to the rest of the world.

$$(VN)_{n,t} = (GN)_{n,t} + (FN)_{n,t} - (VX)_{n,t} \tag{6.25}$$

Gross national product is defined as the sum of total consumption, investment, and petroleum and nonpetroleum exports, less imports and net factor payments to the rest of the world.

$$(GN)_{n,t} = (IT)_{n,t} + (CT)_{n,t} + (XN)_{n,t} + (VX)_{n,t} - (MT)_{n,t} - (FN)_{n,t} \tag{6.26}$$

The balance-of-payments equation balances between imports and exports of goods, services, and capital.

$$(XN)_{n,t} + (VX)_{n,t} - (FN)_{n,t} = (MT)_{n,t} + \sum_i \sum_j (XC)_{i,j,t} \qquad (6.27)$$

where i and j are defined as flow of capital from an OPEC country i to an OPEC country j. The net capital flow XC represents the difference between the capital flow to and from a particular OPEC member country. It also includes capital flow to other OPEC member countries used as side payments to solidify OPEC by maintaining its price and production strategies.

Policy Constraints

The policy equations are not part of the structure of the model per se. They are a mechanism by which the developmental and energy policies of the OPEC member countries and oil-importing countries are included in the model. They can be used for parametric analysis by assuming alternative values corresponding to certain policies. Equation (6.28), for example, states that current-year investment should be less than $(1 + m)$ multiple of that for the preceding year. In other words, $1 + m$ is the investment policy variable.

$$(IT)_{n,t} \le (1 + m)(IT)_{n,t-1} \qquad (6.28)$$

Initially, $1 + m$ is assigned a high value so that it will not be a binding constraint to the model; then growth rates of consumption, GNP, imports, and other components of the economy are measured. Then $1 + m$ could be assigned different values, and the impact of these changes on investment and the various economic indicators could be again measured. In this book, however, only initial values for parameters have been used. Other policy constraints play a similar role in the model.

The utility objective function defined in this model represents the policy goals of individual OPEC member countries. However, certain goals can be formulated only in terms of absolute targets and must therefore be expressed as constraints of the model. One such goal is to maintain per capita consumption at levels at least equal to those of a recent period. This can be achieved by including a constraint requiring total consumption to grow at least as rapidly as population.[17]

$$(CT)_{n,t} \ge (1 + p)(CT)_{n,t-1} \qquad (6.29)$$

Another policy constraint is that no more than a certain percentage of revenue (h) from oil can be invested in foreign countries. Capital outflow will be limited to that percentage even though the rate of return on foreign investment is greater than the marginal efficiency of capital in domestic projects. Such policies are sometimes necessary because of the side benefits of domestic investment for the welfare of the country.

$$(XC)_{n,t} \leq (h)(TP)_{n,t} \tag{6.30}$$

For technical reasons, it is also necessary to place a lower bound on the growth of investment to prevent an unrealistic decline in investment. It is hypothesized that the total investment should be equal to or greater than that for the preceding period.[17]

$$(IT)_{n,t} \geq (IT)_{n,t-1} \tag{6.31}$$

The final policy equation is used to examine whether the sum of individual OPEC country oil production is less than or greater than what has been demanded from it. Initially, the inequality looks as follows:

$$(ED)_t \geq \sum_{n=1}^{N} (XP)_{n,t} \tag{6.32}$$

This inequality can test the stability gap and zero gap. If the inequality holds, OPEC is stable. If, instead, the equality constraint is binding, the implication is that a destruction gap would exist in the absence of equation (6.32). To determine the size of the destruction gap, the "greater than or equal to" sign is changed to a "less than or equal to" sign, and the model is resolved. A comparison of individual OPEC country oil production in the less-than situation and in the equality situation indicates the scope and magnitude of the prorationing program required to ensure OPEC's stability.

7

Estimation and Application of OPEC Oil Supply Model

The first section of this chapter presents the estimated coefficients and values of selected input parameters for the OPEC oil supply model. They are used to determine OPEC's price and production strategy as that strategy is affected by the absorptive capacities of member countries. The price and production strategy is presented in the second section. All values should be considered preliminary.

Input Parameters

The parameters of the objective function are wt, i, and β. These parameters could vary for each OPEC member country for each year of the planning period. However, it is more practical to assume that some of these parameters remain constant between 1976 and 1981, which is a relatively short planning period. The values selected for the parameters represent values based on the present analysis of relevant markets. wt is the weight assigned to each country and time period, and it represents the relative size of oil reserves, military power, population, and other subjective factors influencing the strength of one country with respect to other OPEC members. In this study, the value of wt is assumed to be 1 for all countries and time periods. The value of wt could be changed in future sensitivity analyses to reflect the uneven economic and political strength among the OPEC member countries in influencing price and production strategies. Another parameter is i. It reflects the discount rate for calculating the present value of OPEC's future consumption. The discount rate is assumed to be 10 percent but could be assigned different values in future simulations. The parameter β is the weight for terminal-year GNP. It reflects the postplan growth rate, rate of discount of postplan consumption, and the marginal saving rate. The value of β is initially assumed to be 8. This value was obtained by assuming the following values for parameters in the terminal condition of the objective function: $\delta = 1$, $\alpha = 0.24$, $\zeta = 0.10$, $d = 0.12$, $\infty = 50$, and $T = 10$.

The coefficients of the macroeconometric models for the following nine OPEC member countries are estimated using time-series data.

Code	Country	Code	Country	Code	Country
IR	Iran	SA	Saudi Arabia	NI	Nigeria
IQ	Iraq	LB	Libya	VN	Venezuela
KU	Kuwait	AL	Algeria	IN	Indonesia

No econometric model is constructed for the other (smaller) OPEC member countries, namely, Ecuador, Gabon, Qatar, and the United Arab Emirates at present, because of inadequate data. These countries are among the less influential members of OPEC and are assumed to be price takers. They are allowed to produce up to their maximum production capacity.

As discussed earlier, the structure of each national macroeconometric model used for determining price and production strategies as well as absorptive capacity of each individual OPEC member country is similar. Only the coefficients and parameters vary for each country. The estimated coefficients and statistical criteria are presented in Table 7-1. The tables report the statistics for 11 equations for all nine countries. The values of time series used in estimation of coefficients are in billions of units of local currency in 1970 constant prices, and volumes are in millions of barrels per year. For simulation purposes the values of the variables are subsequently converted to billions of U.S. dollars using 1970 exchange rates, and quantities are converted to millions of barrels per day. Each row in the table constitutes an equation in the model. The symbols for the left-hand-side variables are presented at the top of the "country code" columns. The values of the constants and the other coefficients can be observed directly under the name of the relevant right-hand-side variables used in that equation. Ordinary least squares was used to estimate these coefficients. The time periods used for estimation vary among countries, as shown below.

Iran and Nigeria	1960-1972
Iraq and Venezuela	1961-1972
Kuwait and Saudi Arabia	1963-1972
Libya and Algeria	1964-1972
Indonesia	1966-1972

Most of the coefficients presented in these models are statistically significant. There is no need to emphasize the inadequacy and the low quality of the available data for OPEC as well as for other developing countries. Fortunately, the way in which these coefficients are used in the model minimizes the effect of measurement and estimation errors on the final output generated by the model. The econometric models constructed in this study are used as inequality constraints to the linear programming model. This is unlike the conventional use of econometric relationships as equations (equalities). The inequalities have either upper or lower bounds. Such representation implies that an average growth rate of variables in recent years could be substituted for the coefficients which are not statistically significant. These econometric inequalities state that future growth of left-hand-side variables should at least have the same proportional relationship with right-hand-side variables as they had in the historical period. For instance, the equation

$$(MT) = -16.2 + 0.181(GN)$$

is represented as the following inequality in the linear programming structure.

$$(MT) - 0.181(GN) \geq -16.2$$

This relationship simply states that an increase of 100 million rials in Iranian GNP should generate at least 18 million rials worth of imports. Of course, an equality relationship would have forced exactly 18 million rials worth of imports to be generated. The specification of behavioral econometric equations as inequalities is appropriate because the future development of economic infrastructures of the OPEC economies will not be the same as in the past.

Petroleum revenues are expressed as functions of the volume of petroleum exports. The estimated coefficients for petroleum exports represent the historical government revenue per barrel. The OPEC revenue per barrel used in the model differs from those estimated. This change is dictated by changes in government revenue per barrel that have occurred since the end of the estimation period and which are expected to persist during the planning period. The estimated coefficients of the import equations have not been changed and therefore do not reflect the rapid increase in military expenditures in recent years by some OPEC member countries.

Interest income to OPEC governments from foreign investment is treated as part of net factor payments from abroad. The interest rate r associated with such investment is considered to be 15 percent.

The output-capital ratios used are presented in Table 7-2. Depreciation is assumed to be a constant 7 percent of GNP.

The output-capital ratios are assumed to be constant for the planning period, and labor shortages are considered not to be bottlenecks during the next five years. Imported labor and managerial expertise are assumed to satisfy the short-run needs of these countries. These ratios could be changed if alternative estimates are considered superior, or to perform simulation exercises.

Table 7-1
Values and Statistics of Estimated Coefficients of Equations

$IG \geq$	Constant	TP	$D - W$	R^2	$IP \geq$	Constant	GN_{t-1}	$D - W$	R^2
IR	3.219 (0.5)	0.898 (9.5)	1.12	0.88	IR	-3.095 (-0.5)	0.111 (11.5)	1.24	0.92
IQ	0.041 (4.3)	0.263 (5.1)	2.18	0.71	IQ	-0.018 (-0.5)	0.092 (2.3)	1.89	0.62
KU	0.048 (2.7)	0.050 (1.0)	1.95	0.67	KU	0.068 (2.4)	0.015 (0.4)	0.89	0.78
SA	0.117 (0.6)	0.818 (5.3)	1.79	0.75	SA	0.828 (3.4)	0.042 (2.1)	1.19	0.83
AL	0.119 (0.2)	2.973 (6.9)	0.72	0.84	AL	1.715 (2.6)	0.344 (1.0)	1.88	0.59
LB	0.053 (1.3)	0.283 (2.6)	0.69	0.86	LB	0.179 (3.7)	0.054 (1.1)	1.20	0.85
NI	0.148 (5.6)	1.335 (5.5)	1.57	0.69	NI	0.280 (3.3)	0.454 (3.2)	1.07	0.65
IN	20.988 (1.3)	1.430 (10.1)	2.26	0.94	IN	-387.77 (-4.5)	0.222 (8.2)	2.00	0.92
VN	-2.271 (-0.7)	1.894 (1.7)	0.96	0.73	VN	-5.437 (-7.1)	0.301 (15.4)	1.97	0.96

$CP \geq$	Constant	YD	$D-W$	R^2		$FT \geq$	Constant	VP	$D-W$	R^2
IR	74.088 (5.9)	0.728 (26.9)	1.02	0.98		IR	7.464 (1.4)	0.451 (13.3)	1.75	0.95
IQ	0.066 (1.0)	0.753 (6.9)	1.19	0.83		IQ	0.004 (0.2)	0.261 (5.8)	1.17	0.76
KU	0.081 (4.2)	0.453 (11.1)	1.60	0.93		KU	0.013 (2.0)	0.138 (13.1)	1.04	0.95
SA	-0.481 (-0.5)	0.807 (5.9)	2.57	0.77		SA	0.505 (3.6)	0.338 (26.7)	1.73	0.99
AL	10.145 (11.0)	0.148 (2.1)	1.27	0.80		AL	0.098 (2.3)	0.035 (2.7)	0.81	0.67
LB	0.112 (1.9)	0.502 (4.9)	0.99	0.72		LB	0.002 (2.6)	0.032 (5.7)	1.06	0.79
NI	0.769 (6.5)	0.792 (37.2)	1.72	0.99		NI	0.050 (4.3)	0.211 (7.8)	2.10	0.86
IN	1405.60 (11.2)	0.486 (10.6)	2.06	0.94		IN	43.020 (9.1)	0.122 (5.5)	0.68	0.81
VN	3.297 (1.9)	0.727 (12.5)	0.84	0.93		VN	-0.495 (-0.5)	0.387 (4.2)	1.06	0.60

Note:

IG	=	Government investment
TP	=	Total government take from oil
IP	=	Private investment
GN	=	Gross national product
CP	=	Private consumption
YD	=	Disposable income
FT	=	Factor payments to abroad
VP	=	Value of petroleum produced

Table 7-1 (Continued)
Values and Statistics of Estimated Coefficients of Equations

XN =	Constant	VN	D – W	R²	TD =	Constant	GN	D – W	R²
IR	-1.018 (-1.1)	0.032 (18.2)	2.04	0.97	IR	-10.026 (-7.3)	0.038 (17.6)	1.34	0.96
IQ	0.016 (2.24)	0.007 (0.6)	1.18	0.62	IQ	-0.014 (-3.6)	0.032 (7.9)	0.79	0.68
KU	-0.023 (-3.2)	0.107 (6.3)	1.04	0.81	KU	0.0004 (2.3)	0.0001 (0.7)	2.41	0.56
SA	-0.574 (-1.4)	0.200 (2.6)	2.51	0.68	SA	-1.572 (-1.9)	0.391 (6.2)	1.99	0.82
AL	0.016 (0.2)	0.009 (1.6)	1.28	0.77	AL	0.269 (2.1)	0.036 (5.5)	2.09	0.66
LE	0.002 (2.6)	0.001 (1.7)	0.88	0.63	LB	0.005 (1.2)	0.010 (2.4)	0.57	0.64
NI	0.524 (13.1)	0.019 (2.9)	2.01	0.76	NI	-0.249 (-4.2)	0.076 (8.8)	1.73	0.86
IN	25.463 (0.2)	0.074 (1.6)	1.07	0.66	IN	-73.424 (-4.9)	0.039 (8.1)	1.82	0.91
VN	0.063 (0.4)	0.027 (5.8)	1.69	0.77	VN	-2.923 (-5.4)	0.175 (13.2)	1.51	0.94

TI =	Constant	MT	D – W	R²
IR	6.586 (5.2)	0.316 (24.9)	2.21	0.98
IQ	-0.012 (0.4)	0.427 (2.6)	0.64	0.63
KU	0.003 (3.4)	0.019 (4.0)	2.90	0.63
SA	0.077 (1.7)	0.056 (5.1)	1.99	0.73
AL	0.472 (1.2)	0.407 (5.6)	1.77	0.77
LB	0.003 (0.4)	0.160 (5.9)	1.58	0.78
NI	0.034 (0.6)	0.413 (5.3)	1.19	0.67
IN	30.356 (0.5)	0.343 (2.2)	0.88	0.79
VN	0.358 (4.8)	0.120 (11.5)	2.36	0.92

TP =	Constant	XP	D – W	R²
IR	-18.706 (-2.2)	35.272 (11.7)	1.44	0.93
IQ	-0.144 (-1.7)	0.247 (3.9)	1.53	0.61
KU	-0.314 (-2.7)	0.273 (5.7)	1.33	0.78
SA	0.198 (1.6)	0.362 (9.3)	2.63	0.70
AL	-1.253 (-1.5)	3.233 (3.1)	0.88	0.59
LB	-0.109 (-0.8)	0.200 (3.4)	0.63	0.83
NI	0.026 (4.3)	0.731 (9.5)	1.33	0.89
IN	-116.0 (-5.3)	332.57 (9.6)	0.92	0.94
VN	-1.144 (-1.3)	1.161 (4.3)	0.73	0.63

Note:

XN	=	Value of nonpetroleum exports
VN	=	Nonpetroleum gross domestic value added
TD	=	Direct taxes
GN	=	Gross national product
TI	=	Indirect taxes
MT	=	Total imports of goods and services
TP	=	Total government take from oil
XP	=	Quantity of petroleum export

Table 7-1 (Concluded)
Values and Statistics of Estimated Coefficients of Equations

DO ≥	Constant	GN	D – W	R²	MT ≥	Constant	GN	D – W	R²
IR	0.041 (2.1)	0.0003 (10.9)	1.81	0.91	IR	-16.270 (-2.8)	0.181 (20.1)	0.96	0.97
IQ	0.005 (0.6)	0.058 (7.5)	1.29	0.86	IQ	0.101 (2.9)	0.081 (2.2)	1.28	0.58
KU	0.045 (2.2)	0.068 (2.8)	1.34	0.64	KU	0.051 (1.4)	0.178 (4.4)	0.71	0.67
SA	-0.034 (-1.8)	0.014 (9.2)	2.04	0.90	SA	-1.079 (-1.2)	0.391 (6.1)	0.80	0.79
AL	0.015 (3.0)	0.001 (5.5)	2.80	0.79	AL	0.898 (1.3)	0.217 (6.7)	1.20	0.83
LB	0.001 (3.0)	0.017 (5.9)	1.48	0.81	LB	0.316 (0.7)	0.207 (5.3)	0.98	0.76
NI	0.017 (8.4)	0.002 (6.1)	1.62	0.78	NI	0.477 (13.6)	0.035 (6.8)	1.57	0.78
IN	0.048 (2.4)	0.00003 (4.1)	1.67	0.72	IN	-150.64 (-0.7)	0.184 (3.2)	1.11	0.56
VN	0.048 (3.1)	0.003 (8.8)	1.86	0.88	VN	-1.518 (-2.3)	0.208 (13.1)	2.17	0.94

$CG \geq$	Constant	CG_{t-1}	TT	$D - W$	R^2
IR	-7.554 (-3.5)	0.800 (5.9)	0.339 (3.5)	1.53	0.99
IQ	0.025 (1.4)	0.823 (5.1)	0.098 (1.1)	2.08	0.93
KU	-0.001 (-0.1)	0.510 (2.2)	0.246 (3.1)	2.12	0.91
SA	0.277 (1.3)	0.868 (6.4)	0.073 (1.4)	2.64	0.96
AL	4.500 (3.7)	0.297 (0.8)	0.118 (3.5)	2.31	0.77
LB	0.008 (0.4)	1.077 (8.3)	0.040 (0.6)	3.30	0.96
NI	-0.023 (-0.3)	0.534 (1.2)	0.539 (1.5)	2.10	0.88
IN	90.121 (2.5)	0.034 (0.2)	0.581 (5.6)	2.90	0.96
VN	-0.439 (-0.9)	0.566 (1.9)	0.391 (2.2)	2.10	0.95

Note:

DO = Quantity of domestic crude oil consumption
GN = Gross national product
MT = Total imports of goods and services
CG = Government consumption
TT = Total tax receipts by government

Table 7-2
Output-Capital Ratios

Country	O/K
Iran	0.55
Iraq	0.37
Kuwait	0.50
Saudi Arabia	0.59
Algeria	0.31
Libya	0.49
Nigeria	0.78
Indonesia	0.63
Venezuela	0.27

The rates of population growth per year (p) are assumed to be the same as in the historical period. The share of total oil revenues (h) allowed to be invested abroad is unlimited. That is, the model will choose to invest in foreign portfolios or in OPEC economies based on the rate-of-return criterion without an upper limit on the amount of foreign investment. The upper limit for growth in investment (m) is set at 80 percent per year.

Demand for OPEC oil by the oil-importing countries (or oil-importing countries' excess demand) is a main input to the OPEC price and production strategy model. It is derived as a result of the interaction of supply and demand for all energy forms in the oil-importing countries in an equilibrium environment using that part of the world energy model that applies to oil-importing countries and which was described in Part II. These demands were presented in Table 5-15. The OPEC price and production strategy model initially treats these forecasts of demand for OPEC oil at alternative prices as upper bounds and examines whether the sum of individual OPEC country production exceeds these upper limits. (See forecasts by other writers in Table 7-3). If OPEC production does not exceed demand, the differences represent the stability gap. If OPEC production does exceed demand, the size of the destruction gap is measured, and the model generates a production prorationing scheme.[1] This test is carried out for each year of the planning period.

OPEC is assumed to set the price for its oil at $11 per barrel f.o.b. Persian Gulf in constant 1975 U.S. dollars. At this price, the corresponding demand for OPEC oil can be read from Table 7-5 and is 32 million bbl/D in 1980.

Table 7-3

Comparison of 1980 Forecasts of World Demand for OPEC Oil
(In MM bbl/D)

First National City Bank	30.9
W.J. Levy	
Base case	31.4
Variation 1	35.8
Morgan Guarantee	29.5
Irving Trust	24.6
OECD $6.00	32.6
$9.00	23.4
CACI Inc.—Federal	32.8
Gunning, Osterreith, Waelbroeck (in 1973 $)	
$3.21	37.6[a]
$8.19	27.8[a]
This study (OPEC price per barrel in 1975 $)[b]	
$15.00	29.1
$11.00	32.7
$ 9.00	36.3

[a]OECD demand for OPEC oil only.

[b]F.O.B. Persian Gulf. For demand for OPEC oil at different levels of OPEC crude oil prices per barrel, see Table 5-15.

Sources:

First National City Bank, "Why OPEC's Rocket Will Lose Its Thrust," *Monthly Economic Letter,* June 1975 (First National City Bank, Economics Department, New York).

W.J. Levy, "Future OPEC Accumulations of Oil Money: A New Look at a Critical Problem," 1975 (W.J. Levy Consultants, New York).

L. Ganz, "OPEC Expenditures: Size, Timing, Nature, and Beneficiaries," 1975 (Mitchell/ Hutchins, New York).

S.S. Alexander, "Background Paper," in *Paying for Energy, Report of the Twentieth Century Fund Task Force on the International Oil Crisis* (New York: McGraw-Hill, 1975).

OECD, *Energy Prospects to 1985: An Assessment of Long-Term Energy Developments and Related Policies* (Paris, 1974).

CACI, Inc.—Federal, "Medium-term Ability of Oil Producing Countries to Absorb Real Goods and Services" (Arlington, Va.: CACI, 1976).

J.W. Gunning, M. Osterreith, and J. Waelbroeck, "The Price of Energy and Potential Growth of Developed Countries: An Attempt at Quantifications," *European Economic Review,* vol. 7, 1976, pp.

Table 7-4
Production Requirements and Demand for OPEC Oil at $11 per Barrel[a]
(MMbbl/D)

	1975	*1980*		*1980 Gap*
	Demand and Supply	*Demand*	*Production Requirements for Export*	*Stability (+), Destruction (−)*
Iran	5.4	6.3	4.8	+1.5
Iraq	2.2	1.9	2.6	−0.7
Kuwait	2.1	2.9	1.5	+1.4
Qatar	0.4	0.5	0.5	0.0
Saudi Arabia	7.2	9.1	5.2	+3.9
UAE	1.7	1.8	1.6	+0.2
Algeria	1.0	1.0	0.9	+0.1
Gabon	0.2	0.2	0.2	0.0
Libya	1.5	1.6	1.9	−0.3
Nigeria	1.9	2.4	2.3	+0.1
Indonesia	1.3	1.3	1.7	−0.4
Ecuador	0.2	0.2	0.4	−0.2
Venezuela	2.4	2.8	1.8	+1.0
Total OPEC	27.5	32.7	25.40	+6.60

[a]In 1975 U.S. dollars, f.o.b. Persian Gulf.

Results

The results generated by the model are preliminary. Many of the structural and policy parameters are subject to substantial improvement.

OPEC crude oil production requirements generated by the model are compared against the demands for OPEC oil in Table 7-4. Although the production requirements are estimated for each of the OPEC member countries, demand is estimated as a total and then allocated to individual members based on their relative shares in 1975 OPEC production. It should be noted that the stability, destruction, and zero gaps are measured by comparing the demand and production requirements as a whole rather than on a country-by-country basis. The production requirements of Gabon, Ecuador, Qatar, and the United Arab Emirates are estimated based on their present and potential production capacities and general economic needs rather than by the model.

The results presented in Table 7-4 indicate that the cartel will be stable during the period about 1980 if the Persian Gulf price of OPEC oil is set at $11 (in constant 1975 U.S. dollars). At that price, OPEC crude oil export requirements are less than what is being demanded from them by oil-importing countries, and the need for additional OPEC oil revenues is not great enough to create a surplus market for crude oil. The stability gap shows that OPEC will be in a position to exert pressure for prices higher than $11 in constant 1975 dollars and that OPEC as a cartel will remain strong given the assumptions for this simulation. The size of the resultant stability gap would be equivalent to about 6.6 million bbl/D. This implies two things: (1) at that price, OPEC crude oil requirements to support its internal economic development and foreign investment will be less (by about 6.6 million bbl/D) than what is being demanded from it by oil importing countries, and (2) OPEC's need for oil revenues will not be so great as to create a surplus of crude oil in the world.

A further conclusion is that given the size of stability gap in the early 1980s, the high economic rent for oil as a depletable resource, the slow response in developing substitutes for oil, and the increasing demand for OPEC oil, OPEC will be in a position to obtain prices (in real terms) which will be about 50 percent greater in the early 1980s than they are in 1977 while still meeting the demand for OPEC oil by oil-importing countries. This percentage increase is estimated based on the elasticity of demand for OPEC oil and the size of the stability gap presented in the book. The absolute amount of this real price increase is roughly the same as the 1973-1974 increase.

The growth rates in GNP and in imports of goods and services associated with the production levels of Table 7-4 are presented in Tables 7-5 and 7-6. The model does not provide for excessive military purchases by OPEC members since the coefficients for the import equations were based on imports during the historical period from 1960 to 1972. The results of this study are also compared in these tables with forecasts by the U.S. Department of the Treasury[2] and by CACI.[3] The forecasted real rates of change in imports and in GNP in this study are usually roughly similar to those in one or the other of those two studies.

The model generated a stability gap rather than destruction gap. The production prorationing scheme was therefore not implemented. However, it was tested elsewhere with experimental data and is operative.

Table 7-5

OPEC Imports: Historical Values and Forecasted Real Average Annual Growth Rates

OPEC Countries	Billions of U.S. $		Average Annual Growth Rate				
	Treasury	CACI	Treasury		CACI		This Study
	1974	1975	1974-80	1980-85	1975-80	1980-85	1976-81
Iran	8.0	11.11	20.4	5.6	19.7	2.2	14.5
Iraq	3.5	5.80	17.9	8.3	20.1	6.1	13.1
Kuwait	1.5	2.88	14.6	13.5	2.7	5.4	7.3
Qatar	0.3	0.47	12.3	8.5	8.9	7.0	7.4
Saudi Arabia	3.5	5.13	13.5	18.3	12.2	3.8	12.8
UAE	1.6	1.03	16.0	12.1	15.4	8.6	6.9
Algeria	3.7	5.94	9.9	9.0	5.7	3.7	4.8
Gabon	1.4	1.41	—	—	16.5	0.0	7.5
Libya	3.0	4.44	9.6	4.6	6.9	3.5	8.6
Nigeria	2.5	5.39	22.6	8.2	9.9	3.0	9.7
Indonesia	3.9	5.35	15.8	5.5	11.5	9.4	7.1
Ecuador	0.8	1.31	11.1	8.0	15.0	3.1	9.6
Venezuela	4.7	6.60	12.3	5.0	2.4	-0.6	7.5

Source: U.S. Department of Treasury "The Absorptive Capacity of the OPEC Countries," Washington, September 1975. The data from this source are in 1974 U.S. dollars (f.o.b.).

CACI, Inc.—Federal, "Medium-term Ability of Oil Producing Countries to Absorb Real Goods and Services," 1976, Arlington, VA. The data from this source are in 1975 U.S. dollars (C.I.F.).

Table 7-6
OPEC GNP: Historical Values and Forecasted Real Average Annual Growth Rates

Country	Billions of U.S. Dollars 1975	Average Annual Growth Rates, CACI 1975-80	1980-85	This Study 1976-81
Iran	61.67	11.8	1.2	9.2
Iraq	17.80	9.5	9.5	7.1
Kuwait	11.59	3.8	7.8	3.9
Qatar	2.30	4.8	2.0	3.1
Saudi Arabia	31.20	11.3	3.5	8.6
UAE	7.92	7.0	0.5	4.8
Algeria	14.30	3.0	6.6	3.6
Gabon	2.10	8.1	4.7	4.1
Libya	12.95	6.6	3.4	3.8
Nigeria	23.69	9.7	8.9	7.3
Indonesia	28.00	13.0	0.0	7.8
Ecuador	4.34	11.8	3.9	2.1
Venezuela	28.80	3.1	2.4	3.2

Note: GDP rather than GNP is used in CACI study, and dollar values are in 1975 U.S. dollars.

Source: CACI, Inc.—Federal, "Medium-term Ability of Oil Producing Countries to Absorb Real Goods and Services," 1976, Arlington, Va.

Part IV
World Energy Model: Summary of the
Analytical Approach and Conclusions

8 Summary and Conclusions

This book presents an integrating framework and model for comprehensive analysis of world energy markets. The results generated with use of the model indicate that OPEC will be a viable organization in the years 1980 and 1985 and that it will continue to dictate prices and supplies to oil-importing countries in spite of the substantial differences among its members. These results are based on world energy model simulation of the effects of a set of assumed future developments. The value of the analytical approach or model developed in this book is that it makes it possible to test alternative assumptions on a detailed geographic and type of energy basis. The approach encompasses the entire world and all forms of energy and also incorporates individual OPEC member behavior in a way which not only is realistic but which also preserves those differences among members which could lead either to internal conflict and disintegration of OPEC or to its further strengthening.

Summary of the Analytical Approach

The world energy model determines equilibrium energy prices and quantities in various regions of the world, including the price and demand for OPEC oil. The model does so through interresource substitution of alternative primary energy forms and interfuel competition of final energy products in the oil-importing countries. By incorporating OPEC member countries' absorptive capacities into the model as functions of the macroeconomic structures and growth of their economies, the crude oil price and production strategies of these countries are determined. The model also provides for the flow of OPEC member countries' investments to non-OPEC countries. Further, the model generates a production prorating scheme in the event that OPEC member countries would otherwise collectively produce more oil than what has actually been demanded from them by oil-importing countries. It also allows for the establishment of a joint OPEC fund to be used for side payments (in terms of very low-interest-rate loans) to members in order to discourage them from producing more than their production ration.

On the one hand, development of alternative energy resources and technologies to meet energy requirements is heavily influenced by OPEC crude oil and natural gas price and production strategies. On the other hand, OPEC has repeatedly emphasized that crude oil prices should be set in parity with prices of liquefied hydrocarbons developed from coal, shale oil, etc.

The equilibrium price and quantity which are consistent with both OPEC's general pricing policy and the development of alternative energy resources and technology by oil-importing countries can be determined only by the simultaneous interaction of demand for energy and the supply of energy and alternative energy technologies. That part of the world energy model which deals with oil-importing countries (Part II) provides a methodology for determining this price and quantity. It also determines the flow of energy among regions and each region's demand for OPEC oil in a market clearing environment.

This part of the model can also be used to examine the impact of various policy decisions by oil-importing countries on energy supply, conversion technologies, prices, and demand. The impact of energy conservation and crude oil stockpiling policies, tax policies, oil import programs, and oil embargoes on energy prices, supplies, and demand in each energy sector and geographic region and on the stability of OPEC can be determined.

This part of the world energy model, which deals with oil-importing countries, consists of several models. First are the econometric energy demand models for the various final energy products and regions. The inputs to these models are selected, econometrically estimated coefficients and the values for exogenous variables. The outputs of the models are the demands for final energy products. The second group of models consists of refinery and conversion models. The refineries in each region are represented through a composite refinery model formulated in terms of a linear program. The inputs to the refinery models are various types of domestic and imported crude oils. Each crude oil is represented by its physical characteristics, availability, and cost. Other inputs to the refinery models are the existing capacity and performance characteristics and output fraction of each process unit within the refineries. The outputs of the model are the product mixes, refining process capacities (existing and to be built), and quantities of crude oil necessary to satisfy the mixes of petroleum product demand. The transportation network is the third group of models. It includes representations of alternative tanker and pipeline modes of transportation between various regions of the world. The inputs to the models are transportation costs, existing capacities of different tanker sizes, and transportation between ports. A fourth group of models consists of energy supply models. These are engineering rather than econometrically estimated models. The inputs to these models are reserve estimates for primary energy by quantity and quality, representation of exploration and production activities, and other engineering information regarding resource developments and recoveries. The output of these models are supply curves, which express the available supply at different levels of minimum acceptable prices for each type of primary energy. Finally, an integrating model brings the above models together, solves them simultaneously through iterative procedures, and generates equilibrium prices and quantities for each energy product for different regions.

The output of the oil-importing country part of the world energy model is the net flow of energy among regions and the demand for OPEC oil by each region. In order to derive the demand curve for OPEC oil, various expected levels of OPEC prices are assumed and inputted into the model. The corresponding world energy flow and demand for OPEC oil are determined for each such price. This procedure generates the demand curve for OPEC oil. This curve is then inputted into the second part of the world energy model, which deals with OPEC member countries, in order to determine OPEC's price and production strategies.

This second part of the world energy model (Part III of the book) provides an approach for dealing with issues that are related to OPEC countries, including their oil price and production strategies and investment policies. This part of the model contains the main features of the OPEC economies: economic infrastructure, oil sectors, investment opportunities, and the economic relationships between members and the rest of the world that affect OPEC's stability.

This part of the model is designed to examine various policy decisions made by OPEC member countries and to measure the impact of such decisions on their resources, economic growth, preservation of exhaustible petroleum reserves, investment opportunities, and stability. Specifically, the model can be used to evaluate the impact of OPEC's price and production strategies on the investable surplus of OPEC countries, world capital flows, the development of alternative energy substitutes, the welfare of future OPEC generations, the world economy, the vulnerability of oil-importing countries, the volume of industrial goods imported by OPEC, and conflict among member countries.

The OPEC part of the world energy model is a dynamic econometric, linear programming model of the oil-exporting countries. Macroeconometric models of the economies of individual OPEC countries are formulated and estimated along with their petroleum sectors. The equations of these models, which are estimated as equalities, are represented as inequalities or equality conditions to the linear programming model of which they are a part. They are constraints of the linear programming model. The linear programming model maximizes the present value of the future sum of the individual OPEC countries' welfare (represented by consumption), subject to the econometric conditions (or constraints) presented for each country. Thus, the model determines the levels of crude oil production and prices which are consistent with the capacity of OPEC economies to absorb oil revenues, as well as other pertinent constraints. The input to the model, in addition to the estimated coefficients, is the total demand for OPEC oil by oil-importing countries, as estimated in the first part of the world energy model. The model allows for production prorationing and/or the establishment of a joint fund to be used to effect side payments in the event that aggregate crude oil production by OPEC member countries is expected to be larger than the amount demanded from them by the oil-importing countries.

The world energy model presented in this book uses a wide variety of state-of-the-art methodologies in modeling world energy markets. It extends beyond this state, however, by developing a unique approach for OPEC countries and by integrating that approach with state-of-the-art approaches for the rest of the world. Further research in improving the model should be directed toward improving methodologies, data, the level of regional and product detail, and technological representation.

That part of the world energy model which deals with oil-importing countries is static. Ideally, it should be dynamic. It assumes a competitive market structure for the oil-importing countries. Although some elements of regulated markets or imperfect competition can be represented for these importing countries by imposing taxes, tariffs, etc., a more realistic representation of less competitive energy markets in the oil-importing countries is desirable.

Energy demand models should be based on highly disaggregated product and regional level of detail. The degree of disaggregation in the energy demand models of this book probably exceeds those of any other model. However, it is possible to disaggregate further. Also, the use of time series instead of cross-sectional analysis in estimating parameters should be considered.

In representing the refining structure of the world energy model, use of mini-model approach rather than the extreme-point approach presently used should be evaluated. Finally, the oil, gas, and coal models used for countries other than the United States should be improved, and more regional and product detail should be included.

That part of the world energy model which deals with OPEC member countries does not suffer from many of the above deficiencies. It determines OPEC's price and production strategies in a dynamic intertemporal environment.

Another potential methodological improvement concerns the simultaneous linkage and solution of the OPEC and non-OPEC parts of the model including the determination of OPEC oil prices.

The inadequacy and low quality of energy data are a major problem in world energy modeling. The quality of data used in the world energy model (excluding the United States) is also poor. Substantial interpolation, extrapolation, and professional judgment are presently required in order to meet the input data requirements of the model.

Given all these limitations, the structure of the model is unique and more realistic for analyzing future OPEC price and production strategies than those presented elsewhere in the literature.

Conclusions

The main conclusion derived from the analysis in this book with use of the world energy model is that OPEC will be a viable organization at least through the early 1980s and that it will continue to dictate prices and supplies of crude oil to oil-importing countries despite substantial differences among the member countries in terms of absorptive capacity for oil revenues, political ideology, price and production strategies, and socioeconomic infrastructure. Specifically, the results indicate that if the Persian Gulf price for oil is maintained by OPEC at $11 to 1980 (in constant 1975 U.S. dollars), OPEC will remain stable. The size of the resultant stability gap would be equivalent to about 6.6 million bbl/D. This implies two things: (1) at that price, OPEC crude oil requirements to support its internal economic development and foreign investment will be less (by about 6.6 million bbl/D) than what is being demanded from it by oil-importing countries, and (2) OPEC's need for oil revenues will not be so great as to create a surplus of crude oil in the world.

A further conclusion is that given the size of stability gap in the early 1980s, the high economic rent for oil as a depletable resource, the slow response in developing substitutes for oil, and the increasing demand for OPEC oil, OPEC will be in a position to obtain prices (in real terms) which will be about 50 percent greater in the early 1980s than they are in 1977 while still meeting the demand for OPEC oil by oil-importing countries. This percentage increase is estimated based on the elasticity of demand for OPEC oil and the size of the stability gap presented in the book. The absolute amount of this real price increase is roughly the same as the 1973-1974 increase.

The size of the predicted stability gap indicates that OPEC oil prices will increase at a rate faster than world commodity prices. Thus, it would not be to OPEC's advantage to adopt an "indexation" pricing policy wherein its crude oil prices rise at the same rate as do world commodity prices.

There are strong indications that the world economy would be as able to adjust to price increases of the magnitude required to eliminate the stability gap of 6.6 million bbl/D as it was to the quadrupling of oil prices in 1973-1974. The same is true for the world monetary system.

The OPEC price increases would reduce the demand for OPEC oil by oil-importing countries and would induce stricter conservation and thus reduce their dependency on OPEC. In the short run, the demand for OPEC oil may also be influenced by means such as filling emergency crude oil stockpiles, changes in oil demand because of weather conditions, or changes in mixes of products required. Such fluctuations are "noise-level" variations, however, and would not significantly affect OPEC's stability, long-term crude oil prices, or the structure of world energy markets.

OPEC price increases will stimulate production of energy supplies through development of alternative energy resources in the non-OPEC member countries. Such a development will occur only if the United States and other oil-importing countries launch a large investment program to develop alternative, costlier energy resources; the prices of other energy resources in the oil-importing countries are brought into parity with OPEC crude oil prices (i.e., consumers pay for energy on a replacement cost basis); and the uncertainties associated with development of alternative resources are minimized through government incentives and support. As a result of OPEC price increases and the implementation of measures by governments of oil-importing countries, development and production of coal, natural gas, and nuclear power will expand significantly. In particular, coal production will be expanded as a source for generating electricity and producing synthetic gases and liquids which are direct substitutes for imported oil and gas. Increased production of natural gas at higher prices is likely in the United States and Western Europe. Nuclear power has the greatest potential as a partial substitute for petroleum to meet world energy demand. The scarcity of uranium reserves, the existence of potential safety hazards, and the fear of proliferation of nuclear weapons may, however, limit the rapid expansion of this energy source on a worldwide basis. Finally, the impact of OPEC price increases on the development of competing energy sources will be greater if OPEC exerts sudden rather than gradual price increases.

In addition to OPEC, other participants in the world energy market will likely benefit from higher OPEC crude oil prices as they did from the 1973-1974 quadrupling of OPEC oil prices. Oil and other energy resource companies will benefit in terms of higher prices for their crude oil, natural gas, coal, and uranium reserves in the non-OPEC countries as their prices are brought close to parity with OPEC prices. The potential OPEC price increases will make it easier for the United States government to implement conservation measures and to develop alternative domestic energy resources. Further, it will strengthen the United States economic position relative to other oil-importing countries because the United States will be relatively less affected by higher oil prices and financial imbalances. Finally, a larger portion of OPEC petrodollar surpluses is expected to be retained in the United States than in other countries.

OPEC controls a large portion of the world oil reserves and productive capacity; and despite some internal conflicts, it has and will continue to set and maintain crude oil prices at a high level. OPEC's capacity to absorb oil revenues, in terms of foreign and domestic investments, imports, and consumption, is a major determinant of the volume of oil it will supply. Another determining factor is the size of the reserves and productive capacity of the OPEC member countries. Finally, the political pressure from the rest of the world on OPEC to act as a swing energy producer at a price set by OPEC and the degree of responsibility that OPEC adopts for the economic condition of much of the world will determine the actual volume of oil it supplies. At present prices, OPEC member countries' income from crude oil production will substantially exceed their revenue needs for internal economic development during the 1975-1985 period. In other words, the actual crude oil production needed to meet revenue requirements for OPEC developmental and related purposes is much less than the revenues that would be generated by the demand for OPEC oil by oil-importing countries. In fact, the analyses reveal that by 1980 OPEC as a whole could cut back production by 6.6 million bbl/D without curtailing its economic development programs or even its foreign investment. Countries such as Saudi Arabia, Abu Dhabi, and Kuwait, whose oil revenue needs are not as great as those of Iran, Venezuela, or Nigeria, could make side payments in terms of low-interest-rate loans to the latter group of countries. Further, the accumulated petrodollar surplus and the return from investment could make OPEC revenue requirements even smaller. Even with a low demand for OPEC oil, aggressive OPEC economic development programs, and continuation of present real crude oil prices, the cumulative OPEC petrodollar surplus in current dollars could reach $300 and $500 billion in 1980 and 1985, respectively.

The role of OPEC excess productive capacity in determining the future stability of OPEC and its price and production strategies is exaggerated in the literature. Such assessments have been due to the fact that excess capacity is expensive to develop in non-OPEC countries and once developed, it is not economical to shut it in. Unlike in the rest of the world, however, crude oil productive capacity in the OPEC member countries, particularly those in the Middle East, can be easily expanded without substantial investment. Thus, one can conclude that OPEC's sense of responsibility to, and political pressure from, the rest of the world will lead it to be a swing oil producer at a price set by OPEC between 1977 and 1985.

This book concludes that OPEC is not a monopoly but, instead, is a noncohesive cartel. Its stability is determined by interaction among member countries and also by factors external to OPEC. Lack of similarity among OPEC members with respect to their absorptive capacity for oil revenues, size of oil and gas reserves, political ideology, economic infrastructure, and price and production decisions is one of the major internal factors which could endanger OPEC stability. The recent short-lived OPEC two-tier pricing episode is indicative of such internal conflict. The use of production programming, uniform pricing, and side payments will contribute to its cohesiveness. The use of discount pricing, or chiseling, will lead to its divisiveness. Historically, the apparent disagreement among OPEC countries with respect to uniform pricing has concerned the magnitude of price increases rather than price increases themselves.

The external factors which negatively influence OPEC stability include development of alternative energy resources on a massive scale or discovery of large new oil reserves outside OPEC. However, the principle of "do not drain one's country first" may enhance OPEC's stability. The International Energy Agency (IEA) emergency stockpile requirements will increase the short-term demand for OPEC oil, and hence increase OPEC's stability. However, the conservation measures proposed by IEA and those voluntarily initiated by each country reduce demand for OPEC oil and hence will have a negative impact on OPEC's stability.

The analysis reveals that the recent two-tier pricing among OPEC member countries is a temporary phenomenon (although it might occur again) and will not affect OPEC's stability. The price increases made and compromises reached at the time of the demise of the two-tier pricing system and shortly thereafter indicate that future OPEC member country differences will be internally resolved. The use of production prorationing, side payments, and uniform pricing virtually ensure the continued stability of OPEC for some time to come.

Notes

Chapter 1
Introduction

1. The thirteen OPEC member countries are Algeria, Ecuador, Gabon (Associate Member), Iran, Iraq, Indonesia, Kuwait, Libya, Nigeria, Qatar, Saudi Arabia, United Arab Emirates (UAE), and Venezuela.

2. U.S. Department of the Treasury, *The Absorptive Capacity of the OPEC Countries* (Washington, September 1975 and its update of June 1976).

Chapter 2
Major Participants in the World Energy Economy

1. The twenty-four OECD member countries are Australia, Austria, Belgium, Canada, Denmark, Finland, France, Federal Republic of Germany, Greece, Iceland, Ireland, Italy, Japan, Luxembourg, the Netherlands, New Zealand, Norway, Portugal, Spain, Sweden, Switzerland, Turkey, the United Kingdom, and the United States.

2. The term *oil-importing countries* is used throughout this book to mean all countries except the communist countries and the OPEC member countries. Communist countries are not explicitly considered in the analysis presented in this book. The term *producers* in the oil-importing countries includes small, independent oil, coal, gas, and electric utility companies, domestic subsidiaries of international oil companies, and state-owned energy companies, such as ENI of Italy.

3. Most of the petroleum industries in the oil-exporting countries are owned and managed by their respective governments and their national oil companies rather than by private sectors.

Chapter 3
A Framework for Analyzing the World Energy Economy

1. The term *international oil companies* is used throughout this book to mean the international energy companies. This term covers all the interna-

tional companies who have integrated operations in most phases or in a particular phase of international energy trade.

2. *End-use markets* are those sectors of the energy economy which use the energy products for final consumption. These end-use markets include residential-commercial, transportation, and industrial. The utility sector is not an end-use market since most of the electricity it generates is used by other end-use markets rather than by itself. The utility sector is analyzed in the supply and conversion section of the analysis.

3. The end-products considered are gasoline, kerosene, distillate, residual fuel oil, natural gas, coal, LPG, and electricity. These products are discussed in more detail in subsequent chapters.

4. The term *region* or *country* is used interchangeably in the framework. However, in the world energy model itself, certain regions are defined by grouping several countries together.

5. Ali Ezzati, "Forecasting Market Shares of Alternative Home-Heating Units by Markov Process Using Transition Probabilities Estimated from Aggregate Time Series Data," *Management Science,* vol. 21, no. 4 (December 1974), pp. 462-73.

6. The total cost of producing crude oil and natural gas is composed of investment costs and operating costs. Investment costs are equal to exploration costs, including all dry holes, plus development costs. Total operating costs are equal to the sum of overhead expenses, lifting costs, and production and taxes.

7. The *success ratio*—defined as the ratio of the number of new producer wells in a given period to the total number of wildcats drilled in the same period—depends on the average depth to which wells are drilled, geophysical and core-drilling crew time, average size of oil and gas discoveries, and the success ratio in previous periods.

8. Ali Ezzati, "A Computer Simulation Model for Evaluating the Dependency and Bargaining Power of the Oil Producing Countries versus the International Oil Companies," Ph.D. dissertation, Indiana University, 1971.

9. John H. Adler, *Absorptive Capacity: The Concept and Its Determinants* (Washington: Brookings Institution, 1965), p. 5.

10. UN Economic Commission for Asia and the Far East, *Programming Techniques for Economic Development* (New York: UN Publication, 1960), pp. 8-13.

11. Donald A. Wells, *Saudi Arabian Revenues and Expenditures* (Washington: Resources for the Future, Inc., 1974).

12. John N. Bridge, "Absorptive Capacity and Investment Policies in the Arab World," in Ragaie El Mallakh (ed.), *Energy and Development* (Boulder, Colo.: International Research Center for Energy and Economic Development, 1974), pp. 69-70.

13. M.A. Adelman and S. Friis, "Changing Monopolies and European Oil Supplies," *Energy Policy* (December 1974), pp. 275-92.

14. Hollis B. Chenery and Arthur MacEwan, "Optimal Pattern of Growth and Aid: The Case of Pakistan," in Irma Adelman and Eric Thorbecke (eds.), *The Theory and Design of Economic Development* (Baltimore: Johns Hopkins Press, 1966).

15. Morgan Guaranty Trust Company, "Oil: Looking Back and Looking Ahead," *World Financial Markets,* January 21, 1975.

16. Organization for Economic Cooperation and Development, "Medium-term Outlook for Current Balances," *OECD Economic Outlook* (Paris: OECD, July 1975), pp. 78-85.

17. U.S. Department of the Treasury, *The Absorptive Capacity of the OPEC Countries* (Washington, September 1975).

18. Joseph A. Yager and Elean B. Steinberg, *Energy and U.S. Foreign Policy* (Washington: Brookings Institution, 1974).

Chapter 4
Energy Demand and Supply Models

1. The name of the FEA framework is "Project Independence Evaluation System" and is usually referred to as PIES.

2. See Ali Ezzati, "Policy Applications of the FEA World Energy Analysis Model," in *International Energy Analysis,* Proceedings of Seminar on International Energy Analysis, June 9-10, 1975, Rosslyn, Virginia; sponsored by the U.S. Energy Research and Development Administration (ERDA) and the National Science Foundation. Available from National Technical Information Service (NTIS).

3. The author has contributed extensively to the construction of Gulf Oil's corporate planning model. This model is a very large linear programming model with a detailed representation of Gulf's worldwide production, refining, tanker, and marketing operations.

4. See R.J. Dean et al. (Energy Research Unit, Queen Mary College), "World Energy Model: Description and Results," in *Energy Modeling* (London: IPC Science and Technology Press Limited, 1974).

5. Michael Kennedy, "An Economic Model of the World Oil Market," *Bell Journal of Economics and Management Science,* vol. 5, no. 2 (Autumn 1974), pp. 540-77.

6. See Leo A. Rapoport, "Lorendas Project," in *International Energy Analysis,* Proceedings of Seminar on International Energy Analysis, June 9-10, 1975, Rosslyn, Virginia; sponsored by the U.S. Energy Research and Development Administration (ERDA) and the National Science Foundation. Available from National Technical Information Service (NTIS).

7. *1976 National Energy Outlook* (Washington: Federal Energy Administration, February 1976).

8. F. Gerard Adams and James M. Griffin, "Energy and Fuel Substitu-

tion Elasticities: Results from an International Cross-Section Study,''
Mimeo, University of Pennsylvania, August 1974.

9. Ibid.

10. See *1976 National Energy Outlook*.

11. National Petroleum Council, *U.S. Energy Outlook* (Washington:
NPC, 1972).

12. OECD, *Energy Prospects to 1985: An Assessment of Long-Term Energy Developments and Related Policies* (Paris: OECD, 1974).

13. The coal supply model and oil and gas supply model of FEA were originally managed and improved by ICF, Inc. The materials presented on these models are drawn from some of the documentation ICF prepared for FEA under contract but did not include in the *1976 National Energy Outlook*.

14. The so-called minimum acceptable selling price is different from the prevailing spot or long-term contract prices in the market. The minimum acceptable price over the long run covers finding, developing, and operating costs plus the minimum return on investment.

15. The reserves are defined and included based on the following definitions.

	Reserve Base	
	Depth (ft)	Seam Thickness
Bituminous	Less than 1000	At least 28 in.
Strippable	At most 120-150	At least 28 in.
Subbituminous	Less than 1000	At least 5 ft.
Lignite	At most 120	At least 5 ft.

The reserves are segmented into coal supply regions for two reasons. First, transportation costs for coal are significant. By segmenting the reserves into geographical areas, the costs of shipping coal from specific supply regions to specific demand centers can be taken into account. Second, the rank of coal varies significantly across the continent, but remains relatively constant within wide geographic areas.

Overburden ratio is cubic yards of overburden per ton of coal. Stripping ratio is feet of overburden per foot thickness of coal.

16. When the surface mine approaches the limit of the economic strip ratio, underground mining is then adopted. Surface mines and underground mines have a distinct cost differential.

17. See *Project Independence Report* (Washington: Federal Energy Administration, 1974).

18. See John W. Devanney, III, ''The Competitive Equilibrium of a Transportation Network,'' Mimeo, Massachusetts Institute of Technology, 1974.

19. First, initial demand prices (P_t^d) are selected, where t represents the index of iterations and is initially set equal to 1 ($t = 1$). Second, this initial price is used to determine the corresponding quantity demand (Q_t) and to try to satisfy those quantities with the available supply. Third, the optimal values of activities ($\bar{X}_t$) and shadow prices (Π_t) associated with the initial set of demand prices are generated. If (Π_t) is equal to the price (P_t^d), then the system is in equilibrium. Otherwise, establish a new set of prices (P_{t+1}^d) such that $P_{t+1}^d = \Pi_t + 1/2(P_t^d - \Pi_t)$, set $t = t + 1$, and repeat steps two and three until convergence is achieved.

Chapter 5
Input Parameters and World Demand for OPEC Oil

1. F. Gerard Adams and James M. Griffin, "Energy and Fuel Substitution Elasticities: Results from an International Cross-Section Study," Mimeo, University of Pennsylvania, August 1974.

2. This approach is called *extreme-point representation* of the full-scale linear programming refining model. It is an approximation of a submodel solution space via one or more variables, in terms of the solution space of the main model. Generating extreme points involves manipulating the detailed refining model to produce those models of operation which will satisfactorily represent the flexibility of that refining facility. This is accomplished by introducing revisions of raw material costs and/or product prices, or by other manipulative changes in problem statement suitable for introducing that extreme operation.

3. This modeling system was developed by Bonner and Moore, Inc., Houston, Texas.

4. See W.L. Nelson, "Here's a Look at Productivity in Design and Erection of Refineries—1973 and the Future," *Oil and Gas Journal,* May 12, 1975, pp. 100-102.

5. W.L. Nelson, "Refinery Costs Compared throughout the World," *Oil and Gas Journal,* April 26, 1976.

6. AFRA is a method of assessment for charging freight which is being increasingly used in the tanker market. It became obvious in the early 1950s that to base freight charges on single voyage market rates was unfair, especially to large, long-term customers. The London Tanker Brokers Panel provided an assessment, calculated according to specific terms of reference, of the average rate at which all vessels over 10,000-ton summer deadweight were operating on commercial charter during a given period. The terms of reference are revised from time to time when developments within the tanker industry necessitated changes. At present, AFRA is

published on the first of each month, and the assessment relates to vessels on charter and in service during the month terminating on the fifteenth day of the previous month; e.g., AFRA published on October 1 relates to vessels in service during the period mid-August to mid-September.

7. *World scale* refers to the freight scale used in the world tanker market. The objective of the scale is to provide a yardstick which accurately reflects the relationship between one voyage and another on all voyages on which tankers are utilized.

The rates are established by assuming a hypothetical ship (19,500 tons summer deadweight) with certain performance characteristics and a fixed charter cost per day as factors to calculate the cost of carrying a ton of oil on this vessel on a particular voyage. All basic rates are calculated on the same basis, and a "schedule" is built up. By this means the world scale schedule of freight rates provides a basic freight rate for every voyage which tankers are able to perform on a comparable basis.

Chapter 6
OPEC Price and Production Strategies

1. This curve is also referred to as the oil-importing countries' excess demand curve in the economic literature.

2. C. Blitzer, A. Meeraus, and A. Stoutjesdijk, "A Dynamic Model of OPEC Trade and Production," International Bank for Reconstruction and Development, Mimeo, November 1974.

3. Ali Ezzati, "Analysis of World Equilibrium Prices, Supply, Demand, Imports, and Exports of Crude Oil and Petroleum Products," *Journal of Energy and Development,* Spring 1976, pp. 306-25.

4. J. Cremer and M. Weitzman, "OPEC and the Monopoly Price of World Oil." *European Economic Review,* vol. 8 (1976), pp. 155-206.

5. B.A. Kalymon, "Economic Incentive in OPEC Oil Pricing," *Journal of Development Economics,* vol. 2, December 1975, pp. 337-62.

6. M. Kennedy, "An Economic Model of the World Oil Market." *Bell Journal of Economics and Management Science,* vol. 5, Autumn 1975, pp. 540-77.

7. A version of the material presented in this chapter was originally published by the author as "Future OPEC Price and Production Strategies as Affected by Its Capacity to Absorb Oil Revenues," *European Economic Review,* July 1976.

8. See A.L. Danielsen, "Cartel Rivalry and the World Price of Oil," *Southern Economic Journal,* January 1976, pp. 407-15, for support of this statement. See Esteban Hnyilicza and Robert S. Pindyck, "Pricing Policies for a Two-part Exhaustible Resource Cartel (The Case of OPEC)," *Euro-*

pean Economic Review, vol. 8, 1976, pp. 139-54. See also R.S. Pindyck, "Gains to Producers from the Cartelization of Exhaustible Resources," M.I.T. Sloan School Working Paper, May 1976.

9. Mexico has recently expressed its intention of joining OPEC.

10. This could also be stated as follows: demand for OPEC oil is the difference between world demand and non-OPEC supply of *energy.*

11. See Frederic M. Scherer, *Industrial Market Structure and Economic Performance* (Chicago: Rand McNally and Company, 1970), p. 215.

12. See Danielsen, "Cartel Rivalry."

13. See H.B. Chenery and A. MacEwan, "Optimal Patterns of Growth and Aid: The Case of Pakistan," in I. Adelman and E. Thorbecke (eds.), *Theory and Design of Economic Development* (Baltimore: Johns Hopkins Press, 1966).

14. See Chenery and MacEwan ibid.

15. See J.H. Adler, *Absorptive Capacity: The Concept and Its Determinants* (Washington: The Brookings Institution, 1965). See Chenery and MacEwan, "Optimal Patterns of Growth and Aid."

16. High-absorber OPEC member countries are those which have high propensity to import out of revenues from crude oil exports—Iran, Iraq, Algeria, Nigeria, Venezuela, Ecuador, and Indonesia are in this group. On the other hand, Saudi Arabia, Kuwait, Qatar, and United Arab Emirates are classified as low-absorber countries.

17. See Chenery and MacEwan, "Optimal Patterns of Growth and Aid."

Chapter 7
Empirical Analysis of OPEC Oil Supply Model

1. As discussed later in the results section, under the assumptions made in this study, OPEC decisions lead to a stability gap rather than to a destruction gap. The production rationing scheme therefore was not put into effect. However, this feature of the model is tested and is operative.

2. U.S. Department of the Treasury, "The Absorptive Capacity of the OPEC Countries," September 1975, Washington, D.C.

3. CACI, Inc.—Federal, "Medium-Term Ability of Oil Producing Countries to Absorb Real Goods and Services," 1976, Arlington, Virginia.

Bibliography

Articles

Adelman, M.A. "Politics, Economics and World Oil." *American Economic Review* (May 1974): 56-67.

———. "Is the Oil Shortage Real?" *Foreign Policy,* no. 9 (Winter 1972): 69-107.

Adelman, M.A., and Soren Friis. "Changing Monopolies and European Oil Supplies." *Energy Policy* (December 1974): 275-92.

Akins, J.E. "This Time the Wolf Is Here." *Foreign Affairs,* vol. 51, no. 3 (April 1973).

Al-Atraqchi, M.A. "Iraq's Foreign Trade in Relation to Its National Income and Oil Revenues, 1953-62." *Middle East Economic Papers,* 1968: 1-33.

Amid-Hozour, E. "The Crude Oil Supply: The Middle East, Iran, and the Shell Oil Company." *Tahqiqat-e Eqtesadi,* vol. 9, nos. 25 and 26 (Winter and Spring): 31-46.

Anderson, D. "Models for Determining Least-Cost Investments in Electricity Supply." *Bell Journal of Economics and Management Science,* vol. 3, no. 1 (Spring 1972): 267-99.

Balestra, P., and M. Nerlove, "Pooling Cross Section and Time Series Data in the Estimation of a Dynamic Model: The Demand for Natural Gas." *Econometrica,* vol. 34, no. 3 (July 1966): 585-612.

Baxter, R.E., and R. Rees, "Analysis of the Industrial Demand for Electricity." *Economic Journal,* vol. 78 (June 1968): 277-98.

Brown, G., Jr., and M.B. Johnson. "Public Utility Pricing and Output under Risk." *American Economic Review,* vol. 59, no. 1 (March 1969): 119-29.

Carey, J.P.C., and A.G. Carey. "Industrial Growth and Development Planning in Iran." *The Middle East Journal,* vol. 29, no. 1 (Winter 1975).

Chenery, H.B., and L. Taylor. "Development Patterns among Countries over Time." *Review of Economics and Statistics* (November 1968).

Cremer, Jacques, and Martin L. Weitzman, "OPEC and the Monopoly Price of Oil." *European Economic Review,* vol. 8 (1976): 155-64.

Danielson, A.L. "Cartel Rivalry and the World Price of Oil." *Southern Economic Journal,* January 1976: 407-15.

Darmstadter, J., and H.H. Landsberg, "The Oil Crisis in Perspective: The Economic Background." *Daedalus,* no. 4 (Fall 1975): 15-37.

Deam, R.J. "World Energy Modeling," In *Energy Modelling.* Surrey, England: IPC Science and Technology Press Ltd., 1974.

185

Dhrymes, P.J., and B.M. Mitchell, "Estimation of Joint Production Functions." *Econometrica,* vol. 37 (October 1969): 732-36.

Due, J.F., "The Developing Economies, Tax and Royalty Payments by the Petroleum Industry, and the United States Income Tax." *Natural Resources Journal* (January 1970).

Economics Intelligence Unit. "Soviet Oil to 1980." *QER Special No. 14* (June 1974).

Edens, D.G., and W.P. Snavely. "Planning for Economic Development in Saudi Arabia." *The Middle East Journal,* vol. 24, no. 1 (Winter 1970): 17-30.

Erickson, E.W., and R.M. Spann. "Supply Response in a Regulated Industry: The Case of Natural Gas." *The Bell Journal of Economics and Management Science,* vol. 2, no. 1 (Spring 1971): 94-121.

Esmara, H. "Regional Income Disparities." *Bulletin of Indonesian Economic Studies,* vol. 11, no. 1 (March 1975): 41-57.

Ezzati, Ali. "Analysis of World Equilibrium Prices, Supply, Demand, Imports, and Exports of Crude Oil and Petroleum Products." *Journal of Energy and Development* (April 1976): 306-25.

————. "Future OPEC Price and Production Strategies as Affected by Its Capacity to Absorb Oil Revenues." *European Economic Review,* vol. 8 (1976): 107-38.

————. "FEA World Energy Model." In *International Energy Analysis,* Proceedings of ERDA/NSF Seminar on International Energy Analysis, Washington, D.C., June 9-10, 1975.

————. "Forecasting Market-Shares of Alternative Home-Heating Units by Markov Process Using Transition Probabilities Estimated from Aggregate Time Series Data." *Management Science,* vol. 21, no. 4 (December 1974): 462-73.

Felton, J.R. "Competition in the Energy Market between Gas and Electricity." *Nebraska Journal of Economics and Business,* vol. 4 (Autumn 1965): 3-12.

First National City Bank. "Why OPEC's Rocket Will Lose Its Thrust." *Monthly Economic Letter,* June 1975: 11-15.

Fischer, D.; D. Gately; and J.F. Kyle. "The Prospect of OPEC: A Critical Survey of Models of the World Oil Market." *Journal of Development Economics,* December 1975: 363-86.

Gall, L. "The Challenge of Venezuelan Oil." *Foreign Policy,* vol. 18 (Spring 1975): 44-67.

Gorbet, F.W. "Energy Demand Projection for Canada: An Integrated Approach." *Proceedings of the Council of Economics.* New York: American Institute of Mining, Metallurgical and Petroleum Engineers, February 16-20, 1975.

Gunning, J.W.; M. Osterrieth; and J. Waelbroeck. "The Price of Energy and Potential Growth of Developed Countries: An Attempt at Quantification." *European Economic Review,* vol. 7, 1976: 35-62.

Hnyilicza, Esteban, and Robert S. Pindyck. "Pricing Policies for a Two-Part Exhaustible Resource Cartel: The Case of OPEC." *European Economic Review,* vol. 8 (1976): 139-54.

Hoffman, K.C., and D.W. Jorgenson. "Economic and Technological Model for Evaluation of Energy Policy." *Bell Journal of Economics and Management Science,* vol. 8 (Autumn 1977).

Hotelling, H. "The Economics of Exhaustible Resources." *Journal of Political Economy,* vol. 39 (April 1931).

Houthakker, H.S., and S.P. Magee. "Income and Price Elasticities in World Trade." *Review of Economics and Statistics,* vol. 51 (1969): 111-25.

Hudson, E., and D.W. Jorgenson. "U.S. Energy Policy and Economic Growth 1975-2000." *Bell Journal of Economics and Management Science,* vol. 5, no. 2 (Autumn 1974).

Hutber, F.W. "Modelling of Energy Supply and Demand." In *Energy Modelling.* Surrey, England: IPC Business Press Ltd., 1974.

Johnson, H.G. "Alternative Maximization Policies for Developing Country Exports of Primary Products." *Journal of Political Economy,* May-June 1968.

Johnson, M.B., and G. Brown. "Public Utility Pricing and Output under Risk: Reply." *American Economic Review,* vol. 60, no. 3 (July 1970): 489-90.

Kalymon, B.A. "Economic Incentive in OPEC Pricing Policy." *Journal of Development Economics,* (December 1975): 337-62.

Kennedy, M. "An Economic Model of the World Oil Market." *Bell Journal of Economics and Management Science,* vol. 5 (Fall 1974): 540-77.

Khazzoom, J.D. "The FPC Staff's Econometric Model of Natural Gas Supply in the United States." *Bell Journal of Economics and Management Science,* vol. 2, no. 1 (Spring 1971): 51-93.

Kuller, R.H., and R.G. Cummings. "An Economic Model of Production and Investment for Petroleum Reservoirs." *The American Economic Review,* vol. 64, no. 1 (March 1974): 66-79.

Lebanon, Alexander, "An Oligopolistic Model of the World Supply of Crude Petroleum." *Applied Economics,* vol. 7 (1975): 9-16.

Levy, Haim, and Marshall Sarnat. "The World Oil Crisis: A Portfolio Interpretation." *Economic Inquiry,* vol. 13, (September 1975): 361-72.

Linder, W. "Oil and the Future of Iran." *Swiss Review of World Affairs,* vol. 24, no. 5 (August 1974): 22-24.

Mancke, R.B. "The Long-Run Supply Curve of Crude Oil Produced in the United States." *Antitrust Bulletin,* vol. 15 (Winter 1970).

Manne, A.S. "A Linear Programming Model of the U.S. Petroleum Refining Industry:" *Econometrica,* vol. 26, no. 1 (January 1958): 67-106.

McKie, J.W. "The Political Economy of World Petroleum." *American Economic Review* (May 1974): 51-57.

Mikdashi, Z. "Problems of a Common Production Policy among OPEC Member Countries." *Middle East Economic Papers,* December 1969.

M.I.T. Energy Laboratory Policy Study Group. "Energy Self-Sufficiency—An Economic Evaluation." *Technology Review* (May 1974).

Myint, H. "The Demand Approach to Economic Development." *Review of Economic Studies,* vol. 27 (February 1960): 124-32.

Nelson, W.L. "Here's a Look at Productivity in Design and Erection of Refineries and the Future." *Oil and Gas Journal* (May 12, 1976): 100-102.

————. "Refinery Costs Compared throughout the World." *Oil and Gas Journal,* April 26, 1976.

Organization for Economic Cooperation and Development. "The Medium-Term Outlook for Current Balances." *Economic Outlook* (July 1975): 78-85.

Palmedo, P.F. "Energy Technology Assessment: Consideration of Geographical Scale." *Journal of Energy and Development,* (Spring 1977): 207-17

Samuelson, P.A. "Spatial Price Equilibrium and Linear Programming." *The American Economic Review,* vol. 42, no. 3 (June 1952): 283-303.

Schmalensee, R. "Resource Exploitation Theory and The Behavior of The Oil Cartel," *European Economic Review.* vol. 7 (1976): 257-79.

Solow, R., "The Economics of Resources or The Resources of Economics." *The American Economic Review Proceedings,* May 1974, 1-14.

Stiglitz, Joseph E. "Monopoly and the Rate of Extraction of Exhaustible Resources." *American Economic Review* (September 1976): 655-61.

Taylor, L.D., and D. Weiserbs. "On the Estimation of Dynamic Demand Functions." *Review of Economics and Statistics,* vol. 54, no. 4 (November 1972): 459-65.

Thiel, H. "A Multimonial Estimation of the Linear Logit Model." *International Economic Review,* vol. 10 (1969).

Tsurumi, Y. "The Oil Crisis in Perspective: Japan." *Daedalus,* vol. 104, no. 4 (Fall 1975): 113-27.

Visscher, M.L. "Welfare-Maximizing Price and Output with Stochastic Demand: Comment." *American Economic Review,* vol. 63, no. 1 (March 1973): 224-29.

Wilson, J.W. "Residential Demand for Electricity." *Quarterly Review of Economics and Business,* vol. 2, no. 1 (Spring 1971): 7-22.

Books

Abolfathi, F.; G. Keynon; M.D. Hayes; L.A. Hazelwood; R. Crain. *The OPEC Market to 1985,* Lexington, Mass.: D.C. Heath, 1977.

Adams, F.G., and J.M. Griffin. "An Econometric Model of the U.S. Petroleum Refining Industry." In L.R. Klein, ed. *Essays in Industrial Econometrics,* vol. 1. Philadelphia: Economics Research Unit, University of Pennsylvania, 1969.

Adams, Michael (ed.). *The Middle East: A Handbook.* New York: Praeger, 1971.

Adelman, I. (ed.). *Practical Approaches to Development Planning: Korea's Second Five-Year Plan.* Baltimore: Johns Hopkins Press, 1969.

————, and Thorbecke, eds. *Theory and Design of Economic Development.* Baltimore: Johns Hopkins Press, 1966.

Adelman, M.A. *The World Petroleum Market.* Baltimore: Johns Hopkins Press, 1972.

————. *Alaskan Oil: Costs and Supply.* New York: Praeger, 1971.

Alexander, S.S. "Background Paper." In *Paying for Energy: Report of the Twentieth Century Fund Task Force on the International Oil Crisis.* New York: McGraw-Hill, 1975.

Balestra, P. *The Demand for Natural Gas in the United States.* Amsterdam: North-Holland Publishing Co., 1967.

Berrie, T.W. "The Economics of System Planning in Bulk Electricity Supply." In Ralph Turvey, ed. *Public Enterprise.* New York: Penquin Books, 1968.

Bhatt, V.V. "Theories of Balanced and Unbalanced Growth." In Stephen Spiegelglas and Charles J. Welsh, eds. *Economic Development, Change and Promise.* Englewood Cliffs, N.J.: Prentice-Hall, 1970.

Bohi, D.R., and M. Russell. *U.S. Energy Policy.* Baltimore: Johns Hopkins Press, 1975.

Bradley, P.G. *The Economics of Crude Petroleum Production.* Amsterdam: North-Holland, 1967.

Bridge, John N. "Absorptive Capacity and Investment Policies in the Arab World." In Ragaei El Mallakh, ed. *Energy and Development.* Boulder, Colo.: International Research Center for Energy and Development, 1974.

Burrows, J.C., and T.A. Domenick. *An Analysis of the United States Oil Import Quota.* Lexington, Mass.: Lexington Books, D.C. Heath, 1970.

Darmstader, J. "Appendix." In S.H. Schurr, ed. *Energy, Economic Growth and the Environment.* Baltimore: Johns Hopkins Press, 1972.

de Chazeau, M.G., and A.E. Kahn. *Integration and Competition in the Petroleum Industry.* New Haven: Yale University Press, 1959.

Eckbo, Paul L. *The Future of World Oil*. Cambridge, Mass.: Ballinger, 1966.

Energy Policy Project. *A Time to Choose–America's Energy Future*. Cambridge, Mass.: Ballinger, 1974.

E.N.I. *Energy and Hydrocarbons (Energy Yearbook) Statistical Supplement*. 1972.

Farley, R. *Planning for Development in Libya: The Exceptional Economy in the Development World*. New York: Praeger, 1971.

Fenelon, K.G. *The United Arab Emirates: An Economic and Social Survey*. London: Longman, 1973.

Fesharaki, F. *Development of the Iranian Oil Industry*. New York: Praeger, 1976.

Ganz, L. *OPEC Expenditures: Size, Timing, Nature, and Beneficiaries*. New York: Mitchell, Hutchins, 1975.

Ghadar, Fariborz. *Evolution of OPEC Strategy*. Lexington, Mass.: D.C. Heath, 1977.

Glassburger, B., ed. *The Economy of Indonesia: Selected Readings*. Ithaca, N.Y.: Cornell University, 1971.

Gordon, R.L. *The Evolution of Energy Policy in Western Europe: The Reluctant Retreat from Coal*. London: Praeger, 1970.

Griffin, J.M. *Capacity Measurement in Petroleum Refining*. Lexington, Mass.: D.C. Heath, 1970.

Hartshorn, J.E. *Politics and World Oil Economics: An Account of the International Oil Industry in Its Political Environment*. New York: Praeger, 1967.

Hassan, M.E. *Economic Growth and Employment Problems in Venezuela: An Analysis of an Oil-Based Economy*. New York: Praeger, 1975.

Hoffman, K.C. "A Unified Framework for Energy System Planning." In M. Searle, ed. *Energy Modeling: Art, Science, Practice*. Washington, Resources for the Future, 1973.

Hughes, Richard V. *Oil Property Valuation*. New York: Wiley, 1967.

Kaufman, G.M. *Statistical Decision and Related Techniques in Oil and Gas Exploration*. Englewood Cliffs, N.J.: Prentice-Hall, 1963.

Kennedy, M., "An Economic Model of the World Oil Market." In D.W. Jorgenson. *Econometric Studies of U.S. Energy Policy*. New York: North-Holland American Elsevier, 1976.

Klein, L.R. "What Kind of Macroeconometric Model for Developing Economies?" In A. Zellner, ed. *Readings in Economic Statistics and Econometrics*. Boston: Little, Brown, 1968.

Knauerhase, R. *The Saudi Arabian Economy*, New York: Praeger, 1975.

Looney, R.E. *Economic Development of Iran: A Recent Survey with Projections to 1981*. New York: Praeger, 1973.

MacAvoy, P.W., and R.S. Pindyck, *The Economics of the Natural Gas Shortage (1960-1980)*. Amsterdam: North-Holland, 1975.

Manne, A.S. *Scheduling of Petroleum Refinery Operations*. Cambridge, Mass.: Harvard University Press, 1956.

Marshak, T.A. "A Spatial Model of U.S. Petroleum Refining." In A.S. Manne and H.M. Markowitz. *Studies in Process Analysis*. New York: Wiley, 1963.

Mathur, Ashok. "Balanced v. Unbalanced Growth: A Reconciliatory View." In Alan B. Mountjoy, ed. *Developing the Underdeveloped Countries*. New York: Wiley Interscience, 1971, pp. 142-61.

Mikdashi, Z. *A Financial Analysis of Middle Eastern Oil Concessions, 1901-1965*. New York: Praeger, 1966.

————; S. Cleland; and I. Seymour, eds. *Continuity and Change in the World Oil Industry*. Beirut, Lebanon: The Middle East Research and Publishing Center, 1970.

Mikesell, R.F., ed. *Foreign Investment in the Petroleum and Mineral Industries*. Baltimore: Johns Hopkins Press, 1971.

Nelson, W.L. *Petroleum Refinery Engineering*. New York: McGraw-Hill, 1958.

Nurkse, Ragmar. *Problems of Capital Formation in Underdeveloped Countries*. New York: Oxford University Press, 1970.

Pearson, S.R. *Petroleum and the Nigerian Economy*. Stanford, Ca.: Stanford University Press, 1970.

Penrose, Edith T. *The Large International Firm in Developing Countries: The International Petroleum Industry*. London: George Allen and Unwin, Ltd., 1968.

The Petroleum Publishing Co. *International Petroleum Encyclopedia*. Tulsa, Okla.: The Petroleum Publishing Co., 1975.

Russell, M. *U.S. Energy Policy: Alternative for Security*. Baltimore: Johns Hopkins Press, 1975.

Scherer, F.M. *Industrial Market Structure and Economic Performance*. Chicago: Rand McNally, 1970.

Schurr, S.H., et al. *Middle East Oil and the Western World*. New York: American-Elsevier, 1971.

Searle, M., ed. *Energy Modeling: Art, Science, Practice*. Washington: Resources for the Future, March 1973.

Seifert, W.W.; M.A. Bahri; and A. Kettani. *Energy and Development: A Case Study*. Cambridge, Mass.: M.I.T. Press, 1973.

Takayama, T., and G.G. Judge. *Spatial and Temporal Price and Allocation Models*. Amsterdam: North-Holland, 1971.

Tanzer, M. *The Political Economy of International Oil and the Underdeveloped Countries*. Boston: Beacon Press, 1970.

Tesler, L. *Competition, Collusion and Game Theory*. Chicago and New York: Aldine Atherton, 1972.

Tinbergen, Jan, and Hendricus C. Boss. *Mathematical Models of Economic Growth*. New York: McGraw-Hill, 1962.

Turvey, R. *Optimal Pricing and Investment in Electricity Supply*. Cambridge, Mass.: M.I.T. Press, 1968.

Yager, Joseph A., and Eleanor B. Steinberg. *Energy and U.S. Foreign Policy*. Washington: Brookings Institution, 1974.

Zannetos, Z.S. *The Theory of Oil Tankship Rates*. Cambridge, Mass.: M.I.T. Press, 1966.

Dissertations

Anderson, Robert J. "Application of Engineering Analysis of Production to Econometric Models of the Firm." Unpublished Ph.D. dissertation, University of Pennsylvania, 1969.

Ezzati, Ali. "A Computer Simulation Model for Evaluating the Dependency and Bargaining Power of International Oil Companies versus Oil Producing Countries—An Econometric Approach." Unpublished Ph.D. dissertation, Indiana University, 1971.

Fardi Mohsen Amir, "The Macroeconomic Analysis of a Petroleum Export Economy: Iran as a Case Study." Unpublished Ph.D. dissertation, University of Illinois, 1972.

Halverson, R. "Residential Demand for Electricity." Ph.D. dissertation, Harvard University, 1972.

Hoffman, Kenneth C. "The United States Energy System—A Unified Planning Framework." Unpublished Ph.D. dissertation, Polytechnic Institute of Brooklyn, 1972.

Just, J.L. "Impacts of New Energy Technology Using Generalized Input-Output Analysis." Unpublished Ph.D. dissertation, M.I.T., 1972.

Kadhim, M. "The Strategy of Development Planning and the Absorptive Capacity of the Economy: A Case Study of Iraq." Unpublished Ph.D. dissertation, University of Colorado, 1974.

Kennedy, M. "An Economic Model of the World Oil Market." Unpublished Ph.D. dissertation, Harvard University, 1974.

Richardson, J. D. "Constant Market-Shares Analysis of Export Growth." Unpublished Ph.D. dissertation, University of Michigan, 1970.

Tahmassebi, H. "Impact of Collective Bargaining in International Oil Dealings: A Case Study of OPEC." Unpublished Ph.D. dissertation, Indiana University, 1972.

Publications by Foreign Governments and International Organizations

Blitzer, C.; A. Meeraus; and A. Stoutjesdijk. "A Dynamic Model of OPEC Trade and Production." International Bank for Reconstruction and Development, November 1974. Mimeographed.

Democratic and Popular Republic of Algeria. *Petroleum, Raw Materials and Development.* Algiers: Sonatrack, 1974.

Federal Republic of Nigeria. *Third National Development Plan 1975-80*, I, II. Lagos, Nigeria: Federal Ministry of Economic Development, 1975.

IBRD (International Bank for Reconstruction and Development). "Saudi Arabia—An Economic and Financial Survey," Report No. SM/75/157, June 1975.

————. "A Framework for Regional Planning in Indonesia," Report No. 502-IND, August 1974.

————. "The Venezuelan Financial System and the Monetary Policy Instrument." Document No. DM/74/123. Washington, D.C.: IMF Central Banking Service, 1974.

OECD (Organization for Economic Cooperation and Development). "Medium-Term Outlook for Current Balances." *OECD Economic Outlook* (July 1975): 78-85.

————. *Energy Prospects to 1985* vols. 1 and 2. Paris: OECD, 1974.

————. *Energy Policy: Problems and Objectives.* Paris: OECD, 1966.

OPEC (Organization of Petroleum Exporting Countries). *Annual Statistical Bulletin, 1971.* Wien: Bors and Mueller, 1972.

United Nations. "Trade Projections for Iran." In *Trade Prospects and Capital Needs of Developing Countries.* New York: United Nations, 1968.

————. *Programming Techniques for Economic Development.* Bangkok: United Nations, Series No. 1, E/Cn/5351, 1960.

Research Reports, Working Papers, and Pamphlets

Adams, F. Gerard, and James M. Griffin. "Energy and Fuel Substitution Elasticities: Results from an International Cross-Section Study." University of Pennsylvania, August 1974. Mimeographed.

Adler, J. H. *Absorptive Capacity: The Concept and Its Determinants.* Washington: The Brookings Institution, 1965.

Anderson, K. P. "Residential Energy Use: An Econometric Analysis." Rand Corporation, R-1297-NSF, October 1973.

————. "Residential Demand for Electricity: Econometric Estimates for California and the United States." Rand Corporation, R-905-NSF, January 1972.

————. "Toward Econometric Estimation of Industrial Energy Demand: An Experimental Application to the Primary Metals Industry." Rand Corporation, R-719-NSF, December 1971.

AUFS. "Oil Producers and Consumers: Conflict and Cooperation." New York: The Center for Mediterranean Studies, American Universities Field Staff, Inc., 1974.

Baughman, M. *Dynamic Energy System Modelling–Interfuel Competition*. Washington: National Science Foundation, 1972.

————, and D. Bottaro. "Electrical Power Transmission and Distribution Systems: Costs and Their Allocation." Center for Energy Studies Research Report RR-6, University of Texas at Austin, July 1975.

————, and P. Joskow. "A Regionalized Electricity Model." M.I.T. Energy Laboratory Report No. 75-005, December 1974.

————, and F. Zerhoot. "Interfuel Substitution in the Consumption of Energy in the United States, Part II; The Industrial Sector." M.I.T. Energy Laboratory Report No. 75-007, April 1975.

Berman, M. B., and M. J. Hammer. "The Impact of Electricity Price Increases on Income Groups: A Case Study of Los Angeles." Rand Corporation, R-1102-NSF/CSA, March 1973.

Bodin, L.; A. Doernberg; W. Marcuse; Y. Sanborn; and R. Tessmer. "A Study to Assess the Application of Shadow Pricing Techniques to National Energy Resource Planning." Brookhaven National Laboratory informal progress report BNL 19438, October 1974.

Bonner and Moore Associates. *U.S. Motor Gasoline Economics*. Washington, D.C.: American Petroleum Institute, 1967.

Borg, I. Y. "One View of the World's Petroleum Supplies," Lawrence Livermore Laboratory, UCRL-52075, May 1976.

Bridge, John N. "The Absorptive Capacity of the Saudi Arabian Economy: 1970-1980." Unpublished paper, Department of Economics, University of Durham, 1974.

British Petroleum. "BP Statistical Review of the World Oil Industry, 1975." London: British Petroleum Company, Ltd., 1976.

CACI, Inc.—Federal. "Medium-term Ability of Oil Producing Countries to Absorb Real Goods and Services." Arlington, Va., March 1976.

Charpentier, J. P. "Overview on Techniques and Models Used in the Energy Field." Luxemburg, Austria: International Institute for Applied Systems Analysis, Research memorandum RM-75-8, March 1975.

Cremer, J., and M. Weitzman, "OPEC and the Monopoly Price of World Oil." M.I.T., December 15, 1975. Mimeographed.

Debanne, J. G. "A Regional Techno-Economic Energy Supply-Distribution Model for North America." Faculty of Management Sciences, University of Ottawa, July 1975.

Devanney, John W., III. "The Competitive Equilibrium of a Transportation Network." Massachusetts Institute of Technology, 1974. Mimeographed.

El-Mallakh, Ragaei. *Some Dimensions of Middle East Oil: The Producing Countries and the United States.* New York: American-Arab Association for Commerce and Industry, Inc., 1970.

Haring, J., and Calvin T. Roush, Jr. "Weakening the OPEC Cartel: An Analysis and Evaluation of the Policy Options," Federal Trade Commission, Bureau of Economics, R6-15-32, December 1976.

Houthakker, H. "The World Price of Oil: A Medium Term Analysis," American Enterprise Institute for Public Policy Research; Washington, D.C. 1976.

————, and M. Kennedy, "Demand for Energy as a Function of Price." Paper presented to the American Association for the Advancement of Science, February 1974.

————; P.K. Verlerger; and D.P. Sheehan. "Dynamic Demand Analyses for Gasoline and Residential Electricity." Lexington, Mass.: Data Resources, Inc., 1973.

Jacoby, H.D. "Analysis of Investments in Electric Power." Economic Development Series, Center for International Affairs, Havard University, 1967. Mimeographed.

Joskow, P., and M. Baughman. "The Future of the U.S. Nuclear Energy Industry." M.I.T. Economics Department Working Paper No. 155, April 1975.

Just, J.; B. Borko; W. Parker; and A. Ashmore. *New Energy Technology Coefficients and Dynamic Energy Models,* vols. 1 and 2. McLean, Va.: Mitre Corp. Technical Report MTR-6810.

Kyle, J.F., and W.F. Moskowitz. "The Economics of the OPEC Cartel: A Theoretical Discussion." New York University, 1975, Mimeographed.

Levy, W.J. *Future OPEC Accumulations of Oil Money: A New Look at a Critical Problem.* New York: W.J. Levy Consultants Corporation, 1975.

Lyman, R.A. "Price Elasticities in the Electric Power Industry." Department of Economics, University of Arizona, October 1973.

Morgan Guaranty Trust Company. "Oil: Looking Back and Looking Ahead." In *World Financial Markets.* New York: Morgan Guaranty Trust Company, January 21, 1975.

National Petroleum Council. Committee on Oil and Gas Availability. *Petroleum Productive Capacity.* Washington, D.C.: National Petroleum Council, annual reports.

————. *U.S. Petroleum and Gas Transportation Capacities.* A report prepared by the Committee on Oil and Gas Transportation Facilities. Washington, D.C.: National Petroleum Council, 1967.

Pindyck, R.S. "Gains to Producers from the Cartelization of Exhaustible Resources," M.I.T. Sloan School working paper, May 1976.

Rapaport, L.A. "Long-Range Modeling of Worldwide Energy Development and Supplies—Outline of Formulation and Applications." Department of Geological Sciences, Virginia Polytechnic Institute and State University; Blacksburg, Virginia, July 1975.

Scherer, C.R. "Ex Ante versus Ex Post Estimation of Electric Power System Long Run Costs." Presented at the 45th Joint National Meeting of ORSA/TIMS, Boston, Mass., April 1974.

Sweeney, J. "Economics of Depletable Resources: Market Forces and Intertemporal Bias," Mimeo, Stanford University, 1974.

Symonds, G.H. *Linear Programming–The Solution of Refinery Problems.* New York: Esso, 1955.

A Tripartite Report. *Cooperative Approaches to World Energy Problems.* Washington, D.C.: The Brookings Institution.

Wells, Donald A. *Saudi Arabian Revenues and Expenditures.* Washington, D.C.: Resources for the Future, 1974.

Winkler, R.L. "Risk and Energy Systems: Deterministic versus Probabilistic Models." International Institute for Applied Systems Analysis, research memorandum RM-73-2, Luxemburg, Austria, September 1973.

U.S. Government Publications

Agency for International Development. *Africa: Economic Growth Trends.* Washington: Agency for International Development, 1974.

———. *Latin America: Economic Growth Trends.* Washington: Agency for International Development, 1974.

———. *Near East and South Asia: Economic Growth Trends.* Washington: Agency for International Development, 1974.

———. *Selected Economic Data for the Less Developed Countries.* Washington: Agency for International Development, 1974.

DeCarlo, J.A.; E.T. Sheridan; and Z.E. Murphy, *Sulfur Content of U.S. Coal.* Bureau of Mines Information Circular 8312. Washington: U.S. Government Printing Office, 1966.

Duchesneau, T.D. *Interfuel Substitutability in the Electric Utility Sector of the U.S. Economy.* Staff Report to the Federal Trade Commission. Washington: Federal Trade Commission, 1972.

Energy Research and Development Administration. *A National Plan for Energy Research, Development and Demonstration: Creating Energy*

Choices for the Future, vols. 1, 2. Washington: Energy Research and Development Administration, 1975.

Federal Energy Administration. *1976 National Energy Outlook.* Washington: Federal Energy Administration, February 1976.

————. *Quarterly Report, Fourth Quarter 1974.* Washington: U.S. Government Printing Office, April 1975.

————. "Energy Analysis and Forecasting Models." Technical Report 75-19, Washington, October 1975.

————. *The Relationship of Oil Companies and Foreign Governments.* Washington: Federal Energy Administration, Office of International Energy Affairs, 1975.

————. *Financing Project Independence Financial Requirements of the Energy Industries and Capital Needs and Policy Choices in the Energy Industries.* Washington: U.S. Government Printing Office, November 1974.

————. *Nuclear Task Force Report.* Washington: GPO, November 1974.

————. *Oil: Possible Levels of Future Production.* Project Independence Blueprint, Final Task Force Report. Washington: Federal Energy Administration, November 1974.

————. *Oil Resource Task Force Report.* Washington: U.S. Government Printing Office, November 1974.

————. Project Independence Report. Washington: U.S. Government Printing Office, November 1974.

————. *Report of the Inter-Agency Coal Task Force.* Washington: U.S. Government Printing Office, November 1974.

————. *Task Force Report: Natural Gas.* Washington: U.S. Government Printing Office, November 1974.

Federal Power Commission. *1970 National Power Survey,* vols. 2 and 3. Washington: U.S. Government Printing Office, 1971.

————. *Steam Electric Plant Construction Costs and Annual Production Expenses–1968.* FPC S-199. Washington: U.S. Government Printing Office, 1970.

Hiatt, D. B. "Energy Modeling: A Framework and Comparison." U.S. Department of Transportation, Transportation Systems Center, working paper WP-210-U2-100, September 1975.

McKinney, C. M.; E. P. Ferrero; and W. J. Wenger, *Analysis of Crude Oils from 546 Oilfields in the U.S.* A Report of Investigation 6819. Prepared by the Bureau of Mines, U.S. Department of the Interior. Washington: U.S. Government Printing Office, 1966.

National Petroleum Council. *U.S. Energy Outlook.* Washington: U.S. Government Printing Office, December 1972.

Rapaport, L. A. "Outline of Energy Model Criteria and Overview of LORENDAS Model Characteristics." Presented at ERDA/NSF Seminar on International Energy Analysis, Washington, D.C., June 9-10, 1975.

U.S. Atomic Energy Commission. *Potential Nuclear Power Growth Patterns*. WASH 1098, December 1970. Washington: U.S. Government Printing Office, 1971.

———. "Cost-Benefit Analysis of the U.S. Breeder Reactor Program." WASH-1126. April 1969.

U.S. Cabinet Task Force on Oil Import. *The Oil Import Question*. Washington: U.S. Government Printing Office, 1970.

U.S. Congress, Senate. Subcommittee on Antitrust and Monopoly. *The Petroleum Industry*. March 11, 12, 24, 25, 26; April 1 and 2, 1969.

U.S. Department of the Interior. *Cost of the Oil Import Program to the American Economy*. January 1969.

U.S. Department of the Interior, Bureau of Mines. "International Petroleum Annual." Washington: U.S. Government Printing Office, 1974.

U.S. Department of the Treasury. *The Absorptive Capacity of the OPEC Countries*. Washington: September 1975 and update of June 1976.

U.S. Energy Research and Development Administration. "The Nuclear Fuel Cycle." ERDA-33. March 1975.

Index

Absorptive capacity, OPEC, 2, 5, 10, 12,
    34-40, 126, 143-144, 156, 169
Abu-Dhabi, 116
Activity constraints
    arc traffic constraint, 92-97
    capital requirements balance, 92-97
    cat cracking, 71-74
    crude distillation, 71-74
    fuel and quality, 71-74
    material balance, 71-74, 97
    OPEC policy constraints, 148
    premium gasoline quality, 71-74
    production of energy products, 92-97
    refining, processing and transformation of
        energy products, 92-97
    regular gasoline quality, 71-74
    transportation of energy products, 92-97
Adams, F.G., and J.M. Griffin, 52, 104
Afghanistan, 81
Africa, 119
Agenda for future research, 169
Alaskan North Slope, production, 20, 46-48,
    68
Alexander, S.S., 161
Algeria, 116, 151-152, 162-164
Asia, 119
Assets, OPEC, 137, 139, 146
Austria, 81
Average Freight Rates Assessment (AFRA),
    111

Bahamas, 81
Balance of Payments
    deficits, 1, 5
    equations, 147
    national economies, 6
    oil importing countries, 3, 5, 9
Bantry Bay, 81
Base-load electricity generation, 76-78
Blitzer, C., et al., 125
British Petroleum Statistical Review of the
    World Oil Industry, 43, 107
Bunker fuel, 115
Bureau of Mines, 114

CACI, Inc./Federal, 161
Canada, 48, 80, 81, 118-119
Capital flows
    OPEC, 144, 148
    world, 171
Capital goods, OPEC imports, 143
Capital-output ratios, 137, 139, 146, 153
Capital stock, 119, 142
Caribbean/Central America, 48, 80
Cartel

destructive behavior, 134
OPEC, 132-135
theory, 132
versus monopoly market structures, 125
Catalytic cracking, 69-70
C.E.S. production function, 146
Coal
    capital investment, 89
    costs, 3-4
    deep mines, 88
    high sulfur, 89
    liquefaction and gasification, 4-5
    low sulfur, 84
    metalurgical, 89
    mine depth, 88-89
    minimum acceptable prices, 88
    model, 88-91, 173
    operating cost, 89
    other, 49, 121
    overburden ratio, 89
    price elasticity, 105-107, 117
    resources, 7-8, 89-118
    seam thickness, 88-89
    strip mines, 89
    supply curves, 89, 90-91
    surface mines, 88, 89
    transportation, 78-82
    types of mines and extraction, 90
    variable cost, 89
Cobb-Douglas production function, 146
Coking, 6, 68-69
Communist countries, 119
Competition, inter-fuel, 11, 13, 27, 169
Competitive fringe, 127, 131
Conservation, oil importing countries, 170
Consumer surplus, 97-99
Consumer goods, OPEC imports, 143
Consumption expenditures, private OPEC,
    143, 154-155
Conversion, energy, 103
Conversion balances, energy, 92
Conversion technologies
    general, 170
    models, 170
Corporate energy models, 43
Cost index, refinery, 110
Costs
    capital recovery factor, 66
    data in world energy models, 175
    exploratory drilling, 84
    refinery process, 60
    transportation, 111
Cremer, J., 125
Crude oils
    allocation models, 43

199

About the Author

Ali Ezzati is currently associated with the National Center for Analysis of Energy Systems at the Brookhaven National Laboratory. He formerly directed the Energy Economics Studies Group of the MITRE Corporation in McLean, Virginia. Prior to this he was Director's Assistant for International Energy Analysis and Chief of the International Modeling and Forecasting Division of the Federal Energy Administration in Washington, D.C. (now the Department of Energy). He was a senior economist for the Gulf Oil Corporation in Pittsburgh and has also worked as a financial analyst with the Iranian Oil Refining Company in Abadan, Iran. Dr. Ezzati earned the B.S. degree from the Abadan Institute of Technology and the Ph.D. from Indiana University, Bloomington, Indiana. He has contributed many articles on energy-related subjects to leading U.S. and European journals.